The Candlemaking Design Book

THE CANDLEMAKING DESIGN BOOK

by Carol Feder

illustrations by Emmett McConnell
photographs by Alan Breslaw

Franklin Watts, Inc. · New York · 1974

Library of Congress Catalog Card Number: 72-9781
SBN: 531-02668-x
SBN: 531-02414-8 (pbk.)

Printed in the United States of America
6   5   4   3   2   1

CONTENTS

	INTRODUCTION	1
ONE	BASIC METHOD	3
TWO	PROBLEMS AND PRECAUTIONS	12
THREE	HOUSEHOLD-ITEM CANDLES	15
FOUR	ORNATE CANDLES	34
FIVE	WAX-SHEET CANDLES	44
SIX	CANDLES FOR SPECIAL OCCASIONS	60
SEVEN	PAINTED AND DECOUPAGE CANDLES	78
EIGHT	MODERN CANDLES	88
	INDEX	119

INTRODUCTION

There has been a candle explosion in the last decade. Innovations in styles and techniques have created an abundance of lovely, decorative candles. To walk into a candle shop is to enter a sight and smell emporium: the scents waft out toward you as the door is opened, carrying hints of romance in rose and lavender, touches of the exotic in frangipani, and reminders of holiday cheer in bayberry. The colors are dazzling in their seemingly endless variety.

But candles are no longer exclusively gift shop items. Candlemaking for the home craftsman, young or old, has become a major hobby. Craft shops have jumped to meet the demand and offer wide varieties of molds, as well as the raw materials of wax, wicks, and dyes.

One of the joys of a hobby is to create, especially when the creation is a thing of beauty that has been put together out of simple, everyday objects. *The Candlemaking Design Book* offers you the recipes for such creations, with many candles made from items you have close at hand around the house. The section on "Household-Item Candles" starts with milk cartons, works its way through aluminum foil and gelatin molds, then ends up with a waffle iron candle. The "Modern Candle" section will introduce you to the very simple mysteries of how to make lacy ice cube candles and sand and chunk candles, as well as a host of others. The secret of how to reproduce a favorite cut-glass bowl or vase is revealed in "Ornate Candles," along with methods of carving candle wax. A unique section on "Wax-Sheet Candles" shows how candles can be made with wick, wax, dye, and a simple cookie sheet. Candles can be decorated in a great number of ways — with wax, with oil paints, acrylics, doilies, and appliqués, all of which are described in "Painted and Decoupage Candles." It's a lovely touch to have the right candle for special occasions, especially if you've made it yourself: a birthday clown for a child's party, a Christmas Tree candle at holiday time, a jack-o'-lantern out of wax for Halloween — or an ice cream soda candle, just for fun!

Speaking of fun, that's just what you should get from using this book. Fun — and lovely creations to add warmth and beauty to your home.

Carol Feder
New York, 1974

1

BASIC METHOD

WHAT IS A CANDLE?

A candle is a mass of wax surrounding a wick, meant for burning. The basic principle behind a candle is this: the heat from the burning wick melts the wax, which forms a pool around the wick and is eventually evaporated. As the wax melts and is consumed in the light-producing flame, the level of the candle is lowered. More wick is exposed to the air and thus is able to burn.

MATERIALS FOR CANDLEMAKING

WAX

Before 1850 people made candles from animal fats and oils or insect and vegetable waxes. These materials are still available today, but not very desirable to use because they are so expensive. One of these is spermaceti wax, one of the original candle materials, which comes from the oil of a sperm whale. Although it is obtainable nowadays, it is not often used because of its high cost. Bayberry wax has been used in candles since the Pilgrim days and comes from the coating of berries on the bayberry shrub. This grayish green, highly scented wax, popular in candles at Christmastime, can sometimes be purchased at craft stores; or you can make it yourself by a long process of boiling the berries and skimming off the wax. Other somewhat exotic waxes include carnauba and candelilla wax. You might want to use them as additives to harden your wax.

Beeswax, of all the waxes used in the past, is the one still fairly widely used, especially in church candles. The wax comes from the honeybee, which manufactures it to construct the honeycomb; it is extracted by melting or boiling the honeycomb with water, then skimming the crude wax off the top. Beeswax is one of the highest-quality waxes available, because of its high melting point and the fine finish it gives to candles. The candle hobbyist doesn't usually make molded candles from pure beeswax since it is expensive and also rather tacky, which can create problems when trying to get the candle out of the mold. He can, however, use it in a mixture with regular wax.

In 1850 paraffin wax was developed as a by-product of the refinement of petroleum oil. Paraffin wax was originally soft and plastic, with a melting point of about 120°F, so paraffin candles tended to droop in hot weather, to melt very quickly, and to drip excessively. Additives used to harden the wax ranged from the special waxes, such as beeswax, just discussed, to stearic acid, a special hardening ingredient. Modern science has, however, improved paraffin wax so much that you can now generally get it with high melting points, so it needs no additives except those chosen with candle design in mind. It is the best choice of wax for your candles. This high-quality wax may be bought at hobby and craft stores or may be obtained through petroleum products manufacturers.

Household paraffin, found on grocery shelves, is meant for kitchen use, such as making seals for homemade preserves and jellies. Because of its easy availability you may want to use it for your candles, but keep in mind that it has a LOW MELTING POINT, which means the candle will not be sturdy and will probably lose its shape as it rapidly melts before your eyes. In order to strengthen the paraffin wax, you can add beeswax or stearic acid (discussed in the next section) in the following proportions:

1. 50 percent paraffin
   50 percent beeswax
2. 50 percent paraffin
   50 percent stearic acid
3. 70 percent paraffin
   10 percent beeswax
   20 percent stearic acid

If you have remnants of candles lying about the house, your own or store-bought, you might want to melt them down and reuse the wax in a new candle. The problem that may arise is that the various dyes and hardeners already contained in your scraps may cloud the appearance of your new creation. Avoid this by using old wax only in candles to be dyed dark in color.

Commercial high-quality paraffin wax produces the best results in candles, and you can buy it with varying melting points. This means that you, the candlemaker, must have in mind the particular type of candle you want when you choose the wax. For instance, a container candle (wax burned in a glass) requires a wax with a melting point of only 125° - 130°F, while a sturdy molded candle will be more successful with a harder wax, with a 140° - 160°F melting point. Basically, a candle wax with a melting point of 160°F is excellent for most of the candles described in this book.

STEARIC ACID
OR
HOW TO MAKE YOUR CANDLES HARDER

Stearic acid, sometimes called stearine, is a candle hardener derived from animal fats, and it is generally sold in powdered form. Until the advent of paraffin wax, stearine was often used as the sole material (surrounding the wick) in making candles. Since then, stearic acid has been utilized mainly as a hardening agent. Adding it to wax improves your candle in general.

While making the candle harder and stronger, stearine has the effect of raising the melting point, since a harder candle burns more slowly. For example, 1 part stearic acid to 2 parts household (low-melting-point) paraffin wax will make the candle longer-burning because the wax will be more heat-resistant.

Stearic acid makes your candle burn better too, without smoking, sputtering, or dripping. It also makes your colors appear brighter. Visually stearic acid adds opaqueness to a candle; if you use the 1 part to 2 parts proportions indicated above and use untinted wax, the resulting candle will have a snowwhite appearance. If you want a translucent effect in your candle, use stearic acid sparingly — perhaps 2 to 3 tablespoons per pound of wax.

If you have to purchase your wax in a hobby store, read the accompanying instructions, if any, carefully. Frequently you will find that candle wax packaged for hobbyists has already been treated with hardening agents and that any further additions would be overdoing it.

CRYSTALS
OR
HOW TO ADD GLOSS TO YOUR CANDLE

Crystals, candle additives that improve appearance and quality, are made of polyethylene, a synthetic white opaque plastic. Like stearic acid, crystals make candles harder, longer-burning, and opaque. They also improve the gloss of molded candles and, when dye is added to the wax, produce a very densely colored candle. The use of crystals has some drawbacks:

1. They are relatively expensive.
2. They dissolve best in wax heated close to a very hot 220°F and have difficulty in dissolving at lower temperatures.
3. They tend to form accumulations in the wick when the candle is burned. This clogs the wick and reduces the flame size. To compensate, use a slightly larger wick.

The effect of crystals might be achieved by tearing up clear household plastic bags made of polyethylene and dissolving them in the melted wax.

Crystals are marketed in hobby stores under a variety of names; if you decide to use them, 1 teaspoon to 2 pounds of wax will produce the hard, glossy surface desired.

WICK

The wick is the most critical element in determining whether your candle will burn properly, without smoking, sputtering, or dying. The wick must be chosen as to size and type to be in balance with the rest of your candle. If the wick is too small for the diameter, the flame will be drowned in melted wax, or excessive dripping will occur, since the heat from the flame will melt wax faster than it can be evaporated (see figure 1). Another possibility is that the flame will burn down into the candle, creating a deep indentation, and the wick will suffocate from lack of air (see figure 2). On the other hand, if your wick is too big, the candle will smoke, since the flame evaporates the melted wax faster than it can be accumulated (see figure 3).

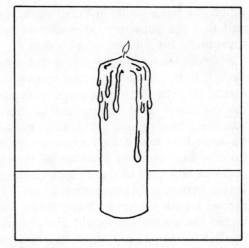

Fig. 1

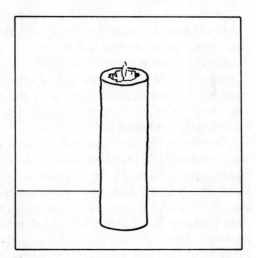

Fig. 2

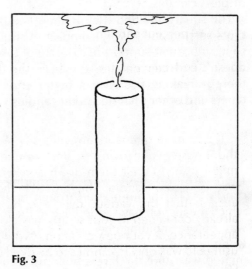

Fig. 3

When you buy wicking in a craft store, you will find that the suppliers list what size wick is appropriate for different-size candles.

Professional wicking is not just a piece of string; it is specially treated woven cotton thread that has been steeped in a salt solution to slow down rapid burning and sputtering. If you don't have regular wicking and can't easily obtain it, here is a recipe for homemade wicks: dissolve 2 tablespoons of salt and 4 tablespoons of borax in 2 cups of water. Soak cotton string in this mixture for 4 hours, then let dry. Cut the proper length for your candle (allow about 2 inches more than the length of the candle so you'll have some slack to work with) and dip the string in melted wax several times; then hang it up to stiffen and dry.

There are three types of wick to choose from.

Metal-core (wire-core) wicking consists of a lead wire surrounded by woven cotton. As the wick burns, the wire melts and the cotton is consumed in the flame. This type of wick is best used in container-type candles, since the metal core holds the wick upright when it is surrounded by hot liquid wax.

The most common type is the flat-braided three-strand wick, made by using three groups of yarn and identified by the number of threads used. The braided wick curls when burned, so that the tip bends into the outer part of the flame, where it is burned off and continually trimmed. This curl puts the flame slightly off-center and can cause dripping and guttering, so don't use the flat-braided wick for tapers and dripless candles.

The square-braided wick is almost square in cross section and is very compact in structure, so it's more self-supporting. The tip of the wick doesn't curl but remains straight in the flame, thereby making this wick a better choice for tapers and other small-diameter candles.

DYE

There are two basic ways of coloring your candle: (1) through-and-through coloring, which means you have added dye to the melted wax before molding the candle; (2) dipping, when you dip a finished candle in colored melted wax until the layers build up a colored shell. No matter which method you decide to use, remember that wax needs oil-soluble dyes.

Oil-soluble dyes, which you can get either at a craft shop or through a chemical company, are available in three forms: powdered, liquid, or color buds. All three types are added to the wax when it is fully melted: the powdered type is stirred in; liquid dye is measured in with a dropper (which, incidentally, makes it easy to reproduce the same colors in successive candles); and color buds, consisting of highly concentrated dye in small blocks of wax, are shaved in small portions until the desired color is obtained. Recently fluorescent dyes for candles have appeared on the market. Some of them come with the caution that they must never be added to wax heated above 170°F, since the fluorescent colors will separate if the wax is too hot, giving the candle an uneven, layered appearance.

Wax is a derivative of oil, which is why you must use oil-soluble dyes. The dyes in food and clothing coloring, as well as in inks, are water-soluble; they will not mix with melted wax. Other homemade coloring agents, such as wax crayons and lipsticks, are filled with acids and preservatives that will accumulate in your wick when the candle is burned, making it sputter and possibly go out. Also, the color in crayons and lipsticks comes from pigments, which do not dissolve in wax, so you will have difficulty in getting a good, even color; insoluble pigments tend to settle in the wax, leaving a candle of varying shades. Oil paints, which have also been used as homemade coloring agents, do work but are very difficult to use, besides being expensive. They take a long time to dissolve in the wax and must be stirred constantly.

If you are caught short of oil-soluble dyes in the middle of a candlemaking session, and you have only crayons or oil paints handy, here is a recipe: 1 medium-sized crayon or 3 tablespoons of oil paint will give color to the amount of wax used in a 1-quart mold.

If you want to test the color of your wax before pouring the candle, put a few drops of the wax on a piece of white paper and let it solidify. Another method is to pour a small amount of wax into a cup of cool water, then press the wax together.

Two things to remember when coloring your candle are that the thickness of the finished candle will determine the intensity of color, and that wax when hardened is always lighter in color than melted wax.

SCENT

A lovely candle is even nicer when it has a lovely scent as well. You should use oil-base scents for perfuming your candle, and they can be bought at craft shops in either liquid or cake form. These scented oils have special ingredients added to help them dissolve in the wax and to improve the burning of the candle.

Your local drugstore is a good source of scented oils, since most pharmacies either sell or can order essential oils. These essential oils, such as oil of cloves, wintergreen, lavender, and patchouli, were once used for homemade medicines, which is why drugstores carry them. They can be mixed with each other to create new scent variations: for example, wintergreen and clove combine to make a spicy menthol scent. Easily available, these oils can be used without any problems as long as you stick to small amounts — at the most, 2 percent of the weight of your candle. If you add too much oil, you run the risk of soot formation and acrid odors.

Don't reach for a regular perfume bottle to add scent to wax, since most perfumes have an alcohol base that is not compatible with wax; aside from producing little aroma, perfume added to hot wax might cause severe spattering. Bath oil, another makeshift way of adding scent, is not recommended, because its fragrance is already diluted. To get a satisfactory odor, you would have to add a lot of bath oil to the wax; too much oil in your candle will cause a mottled, streaky look and would interfere with proper burning.

The scent is absolutely the last thing to add to your wax, which should not be hotter than 190°F at this point. If the wax is too hot, the fragrance oil might burn. Remove the wax from the heat, add the scent, stir well, then pour the candle immediately. Try to use the scent with as little heat as possible for as short a time as possible: the longer scents are exposed to heat, the more they dissipate. Liquid scent should be added with an eyedropper, approximately 10 drops per pound of wax.

A second way of adding scent is to wait until the well in your candle has formed and add the scent, a few drops at a time, at the same time that you refill the well. Also, small slivers of strongly scented wax can be added near the wick of an unscented burning candle to make a strong aroma.

The last way of scenting your candle is to dip the wick in the candle scent before pouring the wax into the mold. This method isn't as good as the others because the wick can't absorb as much scent as wax can, so the odor will be more faint. Moreover, the scent might damage the special treatment that has been given to the wick to aid in proper burning, and your candle might smoke a lot.

Use scent sparingly. It generally lowers the melting point of the wax, so too much scent will harm the rigidity of your candle, as well as cause blemishes in appearance.

5 percent to 6 percent tops for any scent. 3 percent is best.

BASIC STEPS IN MAKING A CANDLE

The first basic step in creating your candle is to prepare your work area. Clear the space of unnecessary objects and spread newspaper all around. Cover the newspaper with waxed paper so that, if any wax is spilled, it can be remelted and reused; if you don't cover the newspaper, any spilled wax will pick up ink and become discolored. Another way of protecting your work area is to use aluminum foil, although this would be more expensive. Don't plan to pour your candle near the kitchen sink; wax that slips easily down the drain when it is hot soon solidifies and clogs the pipes.

Make sure everything you will need is handy; you must never leave a room while the wax is on the stove, even for a necessary piece of equipment. If you must leave, make certain you turn every source of heat off first.

Here is a list of very basic materials:

Melting pot and pan	Wax
Thermometer	Wick
Cooling bucket	Dye
Knitting needle or skewer	Scent
Mold	
Pencil	

1. *Melt the wax.* Wax melts best in small pieces; a large slab of wax can be easily broken up with a few taps of a hammer. Always remember that wax is inflammable — to avoid fire, NEVER pour wax near an open flame. Even heating wax in a pot over direct heat can be dangerous if you let it get too hot. Aside from the possibility of fire, wax can scorch and turn dirty brown if heated too fast or at too high a temperature. To avoid this, the best way of melting wax is in a double boiler, or something similar. To hold the wax, use an old metal pitcher or a large coffee can with a spout squeezed into the rim. Place this container on a trivet in a pan of water over a low flame and wait for the wax to melt (see figure 1). Make sure the container is dry before heating the wax, since water and wax don't mix. Any water left might start to boil when heated and would spatter the wax.

   You should check the temperature of the wax with a thermometer — a metal candy thermometer works well — and never let the wax get over 250°F. It should be poured at differing temperatures, depending on the type of candle you're making. For example, a sand candle works best with very hot wax (230°-250°F) while wax for a milk-carton mold needs to be only 160°F.

2. *Prepare the mold and wick.* While the wax is melting (don't forget to check on it often), you should prepare the mold you are planning to use. It's a good idea to grease the mold with cooking oil or silicone mold-release spray (available at craft stores) to get an easy release of the candle when it has hardened. Many candles require that the wick be placed in the mold before you pour the wax. Most metal molds have a wick hole in the closed end. Thread your wick through this hole and secure it by inserting a screw in the hole from the outside (see figure 2). To make sure no hot wax leaks out, cover the screw and hole with masking or adhesive tape. The other end of the wick should be brought up through the mold and tied around a pencil or bent paper clip at the other end. The pencil should be centered

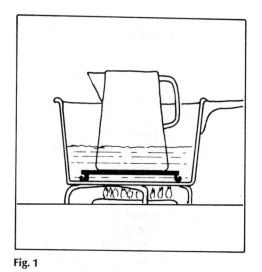

Fig. 1

Fig. 2

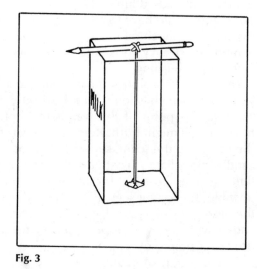

Fig. 3

across the top of the mold. It is very important that your wick be straight up the center of your candle; if it isn't, the burning flame will melt more wax on one side than on the other and will cause lopsided drippings.

If there is no wick hole in the bottom of the mold and you can't easily make one, you can weight one end of the wick with a button or similar object. Tie the other end to the pencil wick holder and lower the wick into the mold. In craft stores you can buy items called wick tabs, which serve the same purpose (see figure 3).

3. *You are ready to pour.* When the wax is fully melted, you can add stearic acid, crystals, and dye, if you wish. If you add too much dye by mistake, don't worry. Just pour off some of the colored wax into a clean container and add some new clear wax to tone down the color. Remember that the scent is the very last thing to add.

It is important to pour your wax from a container with a spout to avoid spilling. Grasp the mold with a towel or potholder to protect your hands, and hold it at a slight angle. Pour the wax slowly down the side of the tilted mold; this prevents air bubbles from forming, which can pit the surface of the candle (see figure 4). If your mold starts to leak, place the bottom in a pie pan with some ice cubes; this will cause the leak to seal in a few seconds.

4. *The water bath.* Let the mold sit for 30 seconds to let all possible air bubbles rise and escape, then immerse the mold in a water bath. The purpose of a water bath is to absorb the surface heat of the wax and produce a glossy finish on your candle. It is easy to make a water bath out of a large plastic or metal wastebasket: just fill it with room-temperature water so that when the mold is put in, the water level comes up to 3/4 inch from the top of the mold (see figure 5). Test the water level before you pour the wax. If you figured wrongly and the water doesn't come up high enough, don't add more water or you will have bubbly lines on the candle. The mold might need a weight on top to hold it down in the water, since wax has a

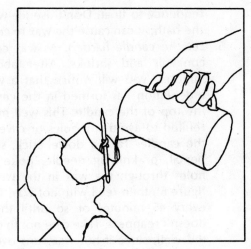

Fig. 4

Fig. 5

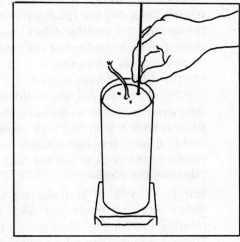

Fig. 6

tendency to float. Don't use ice water in the bath; it can cause the wax to crack.

5. *Let the candle harden.* As wax cools, it congeals and shrinks. After about 45 minutes, you will notice that a well or indentation has formed in the center of the top of the candle. This well must be refilled to avoid any holes or cave-ins in the candle. Take a dowel stick, skewer, pencil, or knitting needle, poke a few holes through the wax in the well (see figure 6), then refill with hot wax. Do this every 45 minutes or so until the well doesn't reappear. Take care not to overfill the well, since if hot wax runs over and gets between the hardened wax and the mold, it will be difficult to release the candle.

The candle should be fully hardened before you try to release it from the mold. Let it cool at room temperature for at least six hours — overnight is best. You can speed up the cooling process by refrigerating the candle, but don't do this immediately or for too long; overexposure to cold can cause cracks in the wax.

6. *Unmold the candle.* When the candle is cool, remove the wick screw, if you've used one, and the wick holder. Turn the mold upside down and tap it lightly on a towel-padded flat surface (see figure 7). If it doesn't come out right away, wait an hour or so, then try again. NEVER bang a metal mold, as any dents will show up on subsequent candles. If you have a lot of trouble releasing the candle, put it in the refrigerator for a while. A last resort is to place the mold under hot running water — this will get the candle out, of course, but the sides will have melted.

With some candles, the mold must be destroyed in order to remove the wax, such as with a glass bottle or paper tube mold. Check the instructions for each candle in the book to see the best way of releasing the candle.

7. *Insert the wick.* If you weren't able or didn't want to insert the wick before pouring the candle, you must do it now. The easiest way is to take a heated metal rod, such as a barbecue skewer or knitting needle and slowly and gently push it

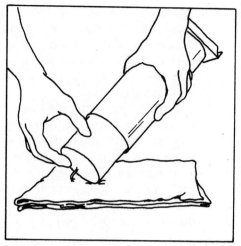

Fig. 7

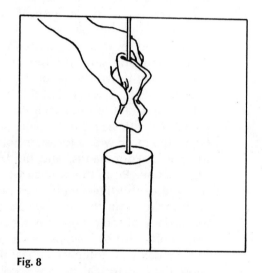

Fig. 8

down through the hardened wax (see figure 8). (Don't forget to protect your hand with a potholder or towel.) It might be necessary to reheat the metal several times before you are finished. If you have an electric drill, the task of making a wick hole is no work at all. Buy an extra-long bit, center it on the top of the candle, and push the button. Dip the wick in melted wax and, when it has hardened, insert it into the hole you've made in the candle. If the hole is much larger than the wick, merely fill it in with more melted wax.

8. *Finish the candle.* There are a few things left to do to make your candle a finished product. Any candle can benefit from being dipped in a clear hot wax bath, which will add a glaze and remove any

rough spots. In order to achieve a high gloss on your candle, the wax for the wax bath should have a low melting point (133°F) and should not contain stearic acid. This is very important, for a higher-melting-point wax will create a dulling film rather than a shine.

The wax for this bath should be very hot (240°F) and in a container deep enough to cover your candle. The double-boiler method can't be used to heat wax for this purpose, since the heat in a double boiler never exceeds 212°F. Use a large kitchen pot over low heat and watch it carefully. Hold the candle by the wick (wear rubber gloves to protect your fingers) and dip it several times in the hot wax. Don't leave it in too long, or the candle will start to melt. A dip in room-temperature water right afterward will add even more shine.

The bottom of the candle will probably be uneven. You can correct this by rotating the candle slowly on a pie pan over a low flame.

If you have a seam line on the candle, take a small knife and run it down the side. You can also polish the candle with a nylon stocking.

A candle over 3 inches in diameter should sit several days before being lighted. If burned too soon, a candle that is not completely cooled will burn rapidly and unevenly.

Remember that you can never fail in candlemaking. If you make a mistake, just remelt the candle and start again.

11

CHAPTER TWO

PROBLEMS AND PRECAUTIONS

PROBLEMS

Every so often you may experience problems with candles you have created. Don't get upset about it, since there is generally a reason for each difficulty and, once you know the reason, you can avoid the problem in the future. Study the following examples for helpful information.

I. My candle won't release from the mold.

    Your wax was too soft. Soft wax doesn't contract as much from the mold wall as does hard wax. If you want to use the same wax, add 10 percent stearic acid.

    You overfilled the well. If liquid wax gets between the hardened wax and the mold wall, it is more difficult to release the candle.

    You cooled the mold too slowly. Use a water bath.

    Your mold might be dented. A metal mold with a dent in it will cause the candle to stick. Avoid dents by handling a metal mold with care; never hit it or bang it.

    Your mold is the wrong shape. Make sure any mold you use, if it is stiff and unbendable, has the opening as its largest part. For example, if you use a glass bottle with a narrow neck, there is no way to slide the candle out once it has solidified; you will have to break the bottle.

    As a last resort to release the candle, run the mold under hot water.

2. My candle has pit marks on its surface.

    You poured the wax too fast, trapping air bubbles inside. Make sure you pour the wax down the side of the mold, slowly.

    Your mold wasn't clean. Dirt and dust particles were inside.

    You didn't use a water bath. The candle cooled too slowly.

3. My candle has cracks or fracturelike lines in it.

    You filled the water bath with too-cold

water. Remember to keep the water at room temperature.

You put the candle in the refrigerator too soon or for too long.

You put the candle in the freezer. NEVER DO THIS.

You used too much scent oil or mold-release oil.

4. My candle has chalky white marks.

    You didn't pour the wax at a hot enough temperature.

    Your mold was too cold. Make sure the mold is at room temperature.

    You took the candle out of the mold before it was ready.

5. Tiny bubbles surround my candle.

    The water level in the bath was not high enough.

    The wax was not hot enough when poured.

    You added more water after the mold was immersed in the bath.

    You used too much scent oil.

6. My candle has caved in on the side.

    You didn't poke and refill the well soon enough.

    The contracting wax forms holes within the candle. Poking and refilling the well avoids these vacuumlike holes, which eventually can cause the candle wall to break down.

7. The wax chips away at the base of my candle.

    You added too much stearic acid or crystals. Too much of a good thing in this case can cause brittleness.

    You left the mold in the refrigerator too long. Too much cold can also cause brittleness.

8. My candle smokes a lot.

    Your wick is too large.

    You are burning the candle in a draft. Keep it away from breezes.

    You added too much scent.

    You don't have a properly treated wick. Trim the wick.

9. My candle drips a great deal; sometimes it goes out.

    Your wick is too small.

    You used wax that was too soft. Soft wax

melts more rapidly than it can evaporate. Add 10 percent stearic acid.

You used a metal-core wick. This kind of wick often causes drippings.

The candle is in a draft.

10. My candle spatters a lot.

    You didn't refill the well. The air in the holes that were left inside cause the wax to spatter when the candle burns down that far.

11. My candle burns unevenly; the wax drips on only one side.

    The candle is in a draft.

    The wick is not centered.

12. When I took my candle out to use it, I found blisters and pimples on it.

    You didn't store the candle in a cool place. At warm temperatures, the air left in the candle combines into small bubbles and rises to the surface. Scrape off the blisters with a small knife and redip the candle in wax heated to 230°-240° F.

13. My candle has become dull and dirty, even before I burned it.

    You should have wrapped the candle in plastic wrap before you put it away. Put a small amount of baby or cooking oil on a soft rag, apply it to the candle, wait a few moments, then polish *GENTLY*. *Or* polish the candle with a nylon stocking. *Or* redip the candle in hot wax or boiling water (the last very quickly indeed!).

PRECAUTIONS

1. Keep small children away from the work area.

2. Make sure you allow enough time. If you are rushed, you might make mistakes or spill wax.

3. Never leave the room while wax is heating. It must be checked often to avoid scorching or burning.

4. Try to avoid direct heat in melting wax by using the double-boiler or pot-in-pan method. Avoid the open flame of a gas stove, if possible, by using electric heat or an asbestos cover over the flame.

13

5. Never pour wax near a sink. When it hardens it will clog the drain. If you accidentally get it down the drain, pour boiling water and liquid soap through the drain (the water will soften the wax and the soap tends to dissolve it).

6. Never pour hot wax into anything that isn't dry.

7 Avoid splashes of hot wax. If you get some on your skin, *immediately* put it under cold running water to make the wax solidify.

8. IN CASE OF A WAX FIRE:
   Never move the pot.
   Turn off the heat.
   Smother the fire with a lid or with baking soda.
   Never use water to put out a hot wax fire; it will only spread the fire.

CHAPTER THREE

HOUSEHOLD-ITEM CANDLES

MILK-CARTON CANDLE

Ingredients:
Wax: paraffin and stearic acid
Wick: flat- or square-braided
Dye: your choice
Scent: your choice
1-quart milk carton
Sharp knife or razor
Masking tape
Flat-bottomed container to hold 2 inches of cold water
Water bath

1. Melt the wax, using the double-boiler method. If you use a full quart carton, you will need about 2 1/2 pounds of wax.

2. Prepare the mold: extra precautions are necessary with milk-carton molds since they tend to bulge from the heat of the wax.

   • Decide how tall you want the candle to be, then cut off the top of the carton with a sharp knife or razor. Make sure you leave enough extra at the top so that you can pick up the carton when it is filled with hot wax. The candle illustrated is 6 inches high, so the carton should be 8 inches high.

   • Clean the carton with cool water and dry thoroughly.

15

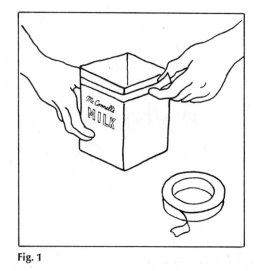

Fig. 1

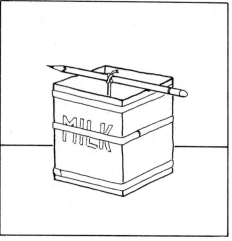

Fig. 2

- Reinforce the carton with masking tape around the top, middle, and bottom. This will reduce the risk of a seam splitting (see figure 1).
- Spray the interior with silicone mold-release spray.

3. Insert the wick. Poke a small hole in the bottom of the carton with a skewer and thread the wicking through. Tie a knot at the loose end and pull it up tight against the bottom of the carton. Cover the knot and hole with masking tape to prevent seepage. Tie the other end around a pencil and center the pencil across the top of the mold (see figure 2).

4. When the wax is fully melted (at least 160°F), add stearic acid at the rate of 2 tablespoons per pound. Add dye according to instructions on page 6. Let the wax cool to 160°F before pouring, since *very* hot wax is dangerous in milk-carton molds. At the last moment, add scent if desired (see page 7).

5. Prepare a flat pan with 2 inches cold water at the bottom and place the carton in it before pouring the wax. This will keep wax leakage at a minimum, since wax will cool and solidify when it hits the cold water.

6. Tilt the carton and pour the wax slowly down the side wall (see figure 3). Let the carton stand upright for 30 seconds to allow air bubbles to rise to the surface.

7. Pick up the carton and place it in the

Fig. 3

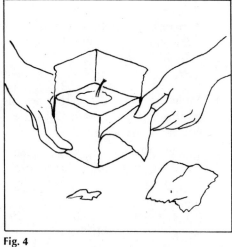

Fig. 4

16

water bath. You must use extreme care as the milk carton is quite fragile when filled with hot wax. Wax is lighter than water; consequently the carton may have a tendency to float in the water bath. Place a book or other object on top of the milk carton to weigh it down.

8. After about 45 minutes, a well or indentation will form around the wick. Take a knitting needle or pencil and gently poke 3 holes in the well. Refill with hot wax. You may have to repeat this procedure 2 or 3 times at about 45 minute intervals as the well re-forms.

9. When the candle is completely cool, tear off the carton (see figure 4). To glaze the candle, dip it in hot clear wax at 240°F (see page 10).

10. **VARIATION:** You can achieve an interesting-looking candle by pressing the sides of the carton together when the wax has hardened somewhat, but is still warm. Retape the carton into the shape you have created.

DOUBLE-WICK MILK-CARTON CANDLE

Ingredients:
Wax: paraffin and stearic acid
Wick: 2 lengths, flat or square-braided
Dye: your choice
Scent: your choice
1/2-gallon milk carton
Sharp knife
Flat-bottomed container to hold 2 inches of cold water
Strong metal clip
Water bath
Masking tape

1. Melt the wax, using the double-boiler method. Allow 5 pounds wax for a 1/2-gallon carton.

2. Prepare the mold: milk cartons are flimsy, so use extreme care in handling them when they are filled with wax.
   • Cut off the top of the carton with a sharp knife.
   • Clean the carton with cool water and dry thoroughly.

3. Clip 2 sides of the carton together at the top with a metal clip (see figure 1).

4. Wrap masking tape around the top, middle, and bottom of the carton. This will reinforce the seams and prevent an unsightly bulge in the middle of the candle. Grease the mold.

5. When the wax is fully melted (at least 160°F), add stearic acid at the rate of 2 tablespoons per pound. Add dye, following instructions on page 6. If you want to fill the well with a contrasting

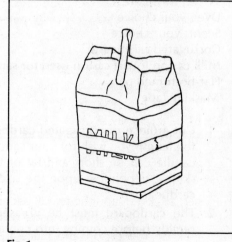

Fig. 1

color, as illustrated, you must reserve a small amount of wax at this point, either to leave uncolored or to dye a second color. Let the wax cool to 160°F before pouring, since *very* hot wax and cardboard do not mix. Add scent at the last moment (see page 7).

6. Prepare a flat-bottomed pan with 2 inches cold water in the bottom and place the carton in it before pouring the wax. This will prevent seepage at the seams, as any wax leaking out will solidify instantly, sealing the leak.

7. Tilt the carton and pour the wax slowly down the side. Let it stand upright for 30 seconds so all the air bubbles have a chance to rise to the surface.

8. Carefully lift the carton into a water bath—the water level should come up to 1/2 inch from the top of the mold (see page 9). Since wax is lighter than water, it has a tendency to float. Weight the carton down with a book if necessary.

9. After about 45 minutes, 2 wells will form in the surface of the wax. Use a knitting needle or a pencil to poke 3 holes in each well. Reheat your wax, or heat the contrasting-color wax you've decided upon, and refill the wells. Do this as

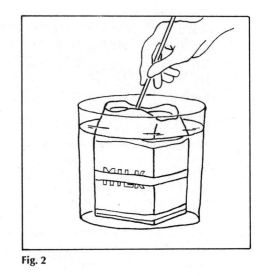

Fig. 2

often as the wells form (see figure 2).

10. When the candle has completely cooled and hardened, remove the metal clip and tear off the carton.

11. Insert the wicking with a heated barbecue skewer (see page 10). Make sure you use a potholder to protect your hands.

12. To glaze the candle, dip it into hot clear wax, at least 240°F (see page 10). Make sure the container for the hot wax is deep enough to cover the candle.

CORRUGATED CANDLE

Ingredients:
Wax: paraffin and stearic acid
Wick: wire-core
Dye: your choice
Scent: your choice
Corrugated cardboard
Milk carton (quart carton used for sample)
Flat-bottomed pan
Masking tape

1. Cut a piece of corrugated cardboard to the length you wish for your candle. The candle can be short and fat or tall and skinny, depending upon the size of the cardboard.

2. The cardboard must be greased thoroughly before coming into contact with wax, since it can be very absorbent.

18

Cover the corrugated side of the cardboard with cooking oil or silicone mold-release spray (see figure 1).

3. Tape the corrugated board together on the smooth side with masking tape and don't stint on the tape; wrap the whole tube very securely (see figure 2). You should now have a hollow tube with the corrugations on the inside.

4. Place the tube into a milk carton, which will serve as an outside brace. A quart milk carton was used for the illustrated example. If the tube is small and fits too loosely into the carton, wrap it with paper before inserting. Put the entire thing into a flat-bottomed pan, just in case of leaks (see figure 3). Don't forget you are working with cardboard!

5. Melt the wax, using the double-boiler method. When it is fully melted, add stearic acid (if it is not already in the wax) at the rate of 2 tablespoons per pound of wax. Add dye according to instructions on page 6. Remember, scent is the very last thing to add before pouring (see page 7).

6. Let the wax cool to 160°F before pouring. First pour only about 1/2 inch of wax into the tube and let it harden. This seals off the bottom and prevents leakage when the mold is filled with hot wax.

7. Suspend a wick in the mold, using either a wire-core wick or one that is weighted (see page 8). Tie the top end of the wick to a pencil and center the pencil across the top of the mold.

8. Pour the rest of the wax slowly into the tube.

9. After about 45 minutes, a well will form in the surface of the wax. Gently poke 3 holes near the wick and refill the well with hot wax. Do this as often as the well forms.

10. When the wax has completely hardened, remove the cardboard by making a slit down the side with a sharp knife and peeling the corrugated board away.

11. To add gloss, dip the candle in hot clear wax, at least 240°F (see page 10).

Fig. 1

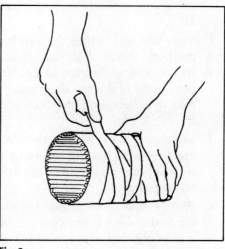

Fig. 2

Fig. 3

19

TWO-WICK CARDBOARD-BOX CANDLE

Ingredients:
Wax: paraffin and stearic acid
Wick: 2 lengths, wire core
Dye: your choice
Scent: your choice
Flat cardboard box
String
Small block of wood
Aluminum foil

1. Take the cardboard box you are going to use as your mold and brace it against seam breakage. Do this by notching the sides of the box at the top and by tying string very securely around it (see figure 1).

2. Melt the wax, using the double-boiler method. When it is fully melted, add stearic acid at the rate of 2 tablespoons per pound (if it is not already in the wax). Add dye, following instructions on page 6.

3. Since cardboard is very absorbent, you must thickly coat the inside of the box with either cooking oil or silicone mold-release spray.

4. Wrap a small block of wood in aluminum foil and place it in the center of the long end of the box. Tape it in place. Make sure the block of wood is at least as deep as the cardboard box (see figure 2).

5. Let the wax cool to 160°F before pouring, since cardboard is not the sturdiest of mold materials. Then pour the wax in all at once until it is level with the edge of the box.

6. After about 45 minutes, a shallow well will form. Poke it with a knitting needle and refill it with hot wax. It will probably not be necessary to do this more than once.

7. When the candle is completely cool, tear off the cardboard box. Level off any uneven spots with a small knife. Carefully remove the aluminum-wrapped block of wood and you will have a candle with 2 places for wicks.

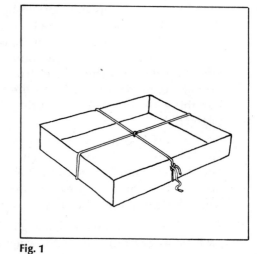

Fig. 1

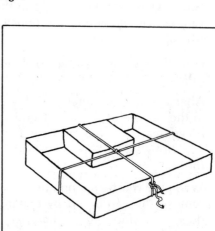

Fig. 2

8. Insert the wicks, using a heated skewer, following instructions on page 10 (see figure 3). Don't forget your potholders!

9. Dip the candle in a hot (240°F) clear wax bath to obtain a smoother finish (see page 10).

10. Two decorating ideas:
   a. Cut shapes out of thin wax sheets (see page 44) and attach them to the candle with hot wax.
   b. Sprinkle powdered dye and torch the candle, using the technique described on page 50.

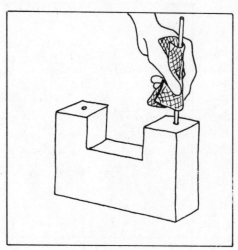

Fig. 3

GLASS-BOTTLE CANDLE

Ingredients:
Wax: paraffin and stearic acid
Wick: flat- or square-braided
Dye: your choice
Scent: your choice
Attractively shaped bottle
Towel
Hammer
Water bath

1. Pick a well-shaped bottle that you think will make a lovely candle. This will be a one-time mold and must be broken eventually to get the candle out.

2. Melt the wax, using the double-boiler method. When it is fully melted, add stearic acid at the rate of 2 tablespoons per pound (if it is not already in the wax). Add dye as instructed on page 6. Add scent at the last minute (see page 7).

3. Warm the bottle under hot running water before pouring in the wax, taking care that no water gets inside. This will reduce the hazard of glass breaking.

4. Let the wax cool to about 165°F before pouring, and use a funnel if the neck of the bottle is narrow. Don't, however, fill the neck with wax, since the glass is generally thickest at this end, making it

difficult to get the candle out without breaking the "wax neck" (see figure 1).

5. Insert a weighted wick (see page 8) into the hot wax and center it on top around a pencil.

6. Lift the bottle carefully into a water bath of room-temperature water.

7. A small well or indentation will form on the surface of the wax as it cools. Gently poke 2 or 3 holes (depending on the size of the neck opening) with a knitting needle and refill with hot wax. Do this as

21

Fig. 1

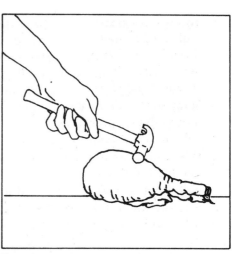

Fig. 2

often as the well forms.

8. After the wax has cooled, remove the glass by wrapping the bottle in a towel, immersing it in cold water, and tapping the bottle with a hammer, just hard enough to break the glass (see figure 2). Be careful not to hit too fiercely or you

will end up with smashed-in spots on the candle. Remove the towel and peel off the pieces of glass.

9. To eliminate any blemishes on the candle, you can dip the candle quickly into either a hot (240°F) wax or hot water bath. See page 9 for details on the hot water bath.

ALUMINUM-FOIL FREE-FORM CANDLE

Ingredients:
Wax: paraffin and stearic acid
Wick: wire-core
Dye: your choice
Scent: your choice
Heavy-duty aluminum foil
Shallow wide-mouthed container

1. Melt wax, using the double-boiler method. When it is fully melted, add stearic acid at the rate of 2 tablespoons per pound of wax (if it is not already contained in the wax). Add dye according to instructions on page 6. If you want to refill the well with a different-color wax, before you add the dye set aside about 1/2 cup of wax, to be either left white or dyed a new color.

2. Take a 12-inch-square piece of doubled aluminum foil and form it into whatever shape you want. Make the bottom of the mold somewhat flat so that the candle will be able to support itself (see figure 1).

22

3. You will need something to support your mold and hold it upright when you pour the wax. A shallow wide-mouthed container would be good, or perhaps a large container filled with sand.

4. Spray the inside of the mold with silicone mold-release spray. This step is not essential, but it is a help.

5. When the wax is at 200°F, pour it *slowly* into the foil mold. If you pour too fast, air bubbles develop.

6. After about 45 minutes, the cooling wax will contract, forming a well or indentation. Poke 3 holes in the well with a knitting needle or pencil and refill it with hot wax. A contrasting color refill, as illustrated, can look very attractive.

7. While the wax in the refilled well is still warm, poke a hole for the wick with a knitting needle and insert a wire-core wick. If your free-form candle is a large one, you may want to have more than one wick.

8. When the wax has hardened and cooled, peel off the aluminum foil (see figure 2). If you want a more even finish on the candle, dip it in clear 240°F wax (see page 10). But be certain that the wick is securely in place before doing so or you might end up holding a piece of wick while your candle slides into the hot wax bath.

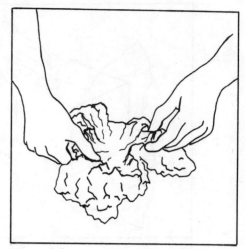

Fig. 1

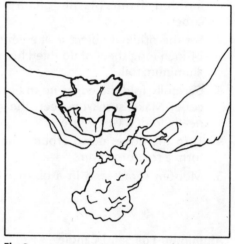

Fig. 2

ALUMINUM-FOIL VARIATIONS

Aluminum-Foil Cube Candle

Ingredients:
Wax: paraffin and stearic acid
Wick: wire-core
Dye: your choice
Scent: your choice
Cube-shaped object
Heavy-duty aluminum foil
Sandbox

1. If you have a cube candle already, use that to shape your mold. If not, any cube-shaped object, such as a small box, will do. The candle in the illustration was

23

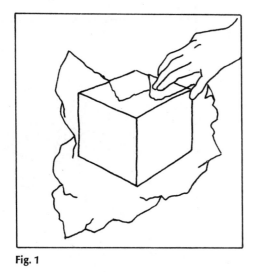

Fig. 1

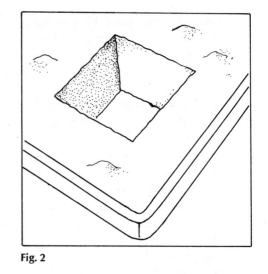

Fig. 2

molded from plastic picture-display cubes.

2. Set the original object in the center of a 24-inch long sheet of doubled heavy-duty aluminum foil.

3. Carefully fold the edges up to encase the cube. Make sure you keep the corners neatly folded (see figure 1).

4. Turn the edges down around the top to form a reinforced rim.

5. Moisten some sand in a dishpan or box until it is damp, but not sopping wet. Mound it into a bed to support the cube.

6. Push the aluminum-foil-wrapped cube into the sand and press the sand firmly against the sides. Then remove the cube, but leave the foil in place. The sand will now act as a support for the foil shape (see figure 2).

7. Continue with the procedures for melting and pouring the wax as described on the previous page.

Aluminum-Foil Sand Candle

Ingredients:
Wax: paraffin and stearic acid
Wick: wire-core
Dye: your choice
Scent: your choice
Heavy-duty aluminum foil
Sandbox

1. Dampen some sand in a dishpan or cardboard box. Shape it into a mound.

2. Cut a 15-inch length of aluminum foil and push it into the sand. As this is a type of free-form candle, you can design whatever shape you like. The candle illustrated was made by pressing a juice bottle into the foil to form a base. The bottle was then lifted out and the foil edges were fluted (see figure 1).

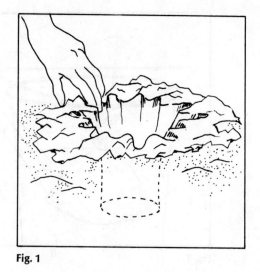

Fig. 1

Fig. 2

3. When you are satisfied with your design, carefully lift the foil out of the sand. If your design has edges that protrude below the general contour of the sides, you might push through the sand when lifting the foil. Avoid this by folding the foil in toward the center before lifting.

4. Continue with the procedures for melting and pouring the wax into the sand mold, as described on page 8, with the exception that the wax should be poured at 230°F in order for a layer of sand to adhere (see figure 2).

PLASTIC-BAG CANDLE

Ingredients:
Wax: paraffin
Wick: wire-core
Dye: your choice
Scent: your choice
Plastic bag
Wire to hold the bag closed
Pail of room-temperature water
Wire coat hanger

1. You will need two people to make this candle because one must hold the bag while the other pours the wax. Also, to be on the safe side, use a heavy-duty plastic bag, since the seams on a lightweight bag might break unless the wax is at a very low temperature.

2. Melt the wax, using the double-boiler method. When it has fully melted, add stearic acid at the rate of 2 tablespoons per pound (unless it is already in the wax). Add dye according to instructions on page 6. Let the wax cool to 160°F before pouring. Add scent at the last minute (see page 7).

3. Prepare to pour the wax by having your assistant hold the bag open for you over a container (pail, pot, sink) of room-temperature water. This is in case the bag

25

Fig. 1

Fig. 2

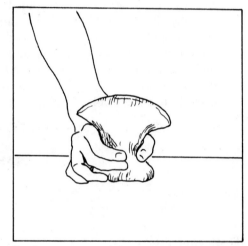

Fig. 3

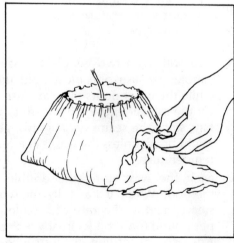

Fig. 4

breaks or in case wax leaks out (see figure 1).

4. Slowly fill the bag with wax and gather the top together. Tie the top with a wire to hold it closed.

5. The in-case-of-leaks container of water is now going to be used as a water bath. Lower the bag into the water and let it cool. You will find that, once in the water, the wax-filled bag will lose its bag shape and become a formless blob under the water. To counteract this, use a wire coat hanger to support the bag; poke a hole through the top of the bag, hang it over the hook of the hanger, and suspend it in the water (see figure 2).

6. **VARIATION:** If you rock the bag gently back and forth when you lower it into the water, wax from the top will come up along the sides of the bag, forming a ridge, which can be quite attractive. If you want your candle to have an unusual shape, mold the bag of wax in your hands while the wax is still warm (see figure 3).

7. After the wax is completely cool, pull off the plastic bag (see figure 4).

8. Insert the wicking, using a heated barbecue skewer or knitting needle (see page 10).

9. You might find that the base of the candle is not level enough to permit it to stand upright. You can flatten the bottom by rotating it slowly on a heated pan.

KITCHEN-MOLD FLOATING CANDLE

Ingredients:
Wax: low-melting-point (134°-140°F) paraffin
Wick: wire-core
Deep container
Eggbeater or fork
Small kitchen mold, such as gelatin or poached-egg mold
Water bath

1. Using the double-boiler method, melt wax that has a melting point between 134° and 140°F. This type of wax whips the most easily and is most appropriate for a floating candle.

2. When the wax has fully melted, add dye according to the instructions on page 6. Do not add stearic acid—since it is not necessary for this candle.

3. Pour the wax into a container that is deep enough so that the wax will not spatter all over the area when you whip it.

4. Let the wax cool until a film or skin forms on the surface (see figure 1). Then, using an eggbeater or a fork, whip the wax until it has a fluffy surface (see figure 2).

5. Lightly oil the mold, either with cooking oil or silicone mold-release spray.

6. When the surface of the wax is frothy, start pressing it into the mold, using your fingers or a fork as a tool (see figure 3).

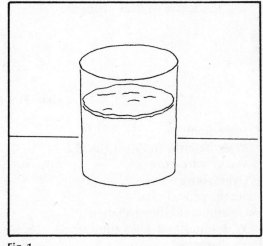

Fig. 1

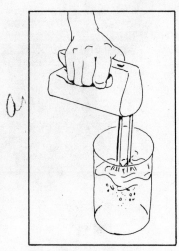

Fig. 2

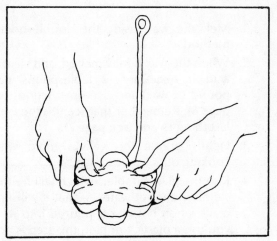

Fig. 3

27

7. Insert a wire-core wick while the wax is still warm (see figure 4).

8. After 10 minutes, place the candle, in the mold, to float in a water bath.

9. When the wax has completely cooled and hardened, gently pull the sides of the mold away from the candle.

10. If the candle doesn't release easily, let it drop a few inches onto a padded surface.

11. Float the candle in a bowl of water to make a lovely centerpiece. Or make several candles and set them adrift in a swimming pool to add atmosphere to an outdoor evening party.

12. **VARIATION:** If you want, instead of using whipped wax in the mold, pour in about 1/2 inch of regular wax. Any more wax than this, and the candle might be too heavy to float properly.

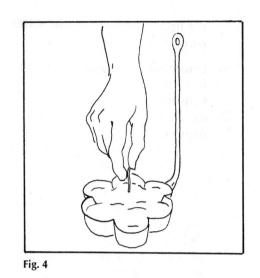

Fig. 4

GELATIN-MOLD MUSHROOM

Ingredients:
Wax: paraffin and stearic acid
Wick: wire-core
Dye: your choice
Scent: your choice
Gelatin mold (bowl-shaped)
Wide-mouthed glass tumbler (3- to 4-inch diameter)
Water bath

1. Melt the wax, using the double-boiler method.

2. When the wax is fully melted, add stearic acid if necessary (2 tablespoons per pound of wax) and dye (instructions on page 6). Remember that scent is the very last thing to add (see page 7).

3. Lightly grease the gelatin mold with cooking oil.

4. Run the glass tumbler (which will be the stem) under hot water so that it will not crack when hot wax is poured into it. If you use a plastic tumbler, this step is not necessary. Whichever you use, make sure it doesn't have an indented rim on

the lip, or you will not be able to get the wax out without breaking the tumbler.

5. Slowly pour the wax, heated to 180°F, into the gelatin mold (see figure 1). If you want a layered mushroom cap, see the instructions for layered candles on page 88.

6. Slowly pour the wax, heated to 160°F, into the tumbler, taking care that you pour down the side of the glass while holding it at a tilt. This prevents air bubbles from forming.

7. After letting the molds stand for 1/2 minute, place both in a warm water bath. Make sure the water doesn't run over the top of the mold, since you don't want any water to mix with the wax. You have 2 molds to cool, so provide a water bath large enough to hold both. Of course, you can use 2 separate containers.

8. When a well appears in the mold and in the tumbler, approximately 30 minutes to 45 minutes later, poke each well with a knitting needle or pencil 3 times and refill with hot wax. If you are using a large gelatin mold, you will have to repeat this process 2 or 3 times. Do not fill the well completely: leave a slight indentation.

9. When the wax has hardened, release it from the gelatin mold by gently pulling the edges of the mold away from the wax. Drop the mold gently onto a padded surface and the wax should fall out. If it doesn't, let it cool longer.

10. Release the wax from the tumbler by tapping it lightly on a firmly padded surface (lay a towel across the kitchen counter).

11. Rub the top of the stem—that is, the part that was at the bottom of the glass—against a heated pie pan (see figure 2); then press it against the flat part of the gelatin-mold wax (see figure 3). If this doesn't hold together, brush both surfaces with hot wax (230°F) and press together again.

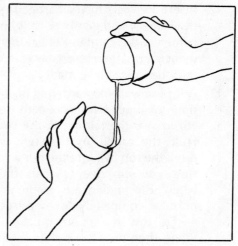

Fig. 1

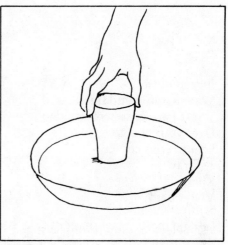

Fig. 2

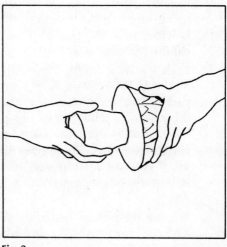

Fig. 3

12. Insert the wick: heat a barbecue skewer, then slowly and gently push it down the center of the candle. Reheat the skewer if necessary. Then insert a wire-core wick into the hole you've made.

13. After the wick has hardened in place, it is time for a quick hot wax bath (see page 10) to seal the joining of the two parts. Hold the candle by the stem end and dunk the top half into the hot wax. Make sure you dip deeper than the place where the joining was made; the joint must be completely covered (see figure 4). Do this in and out quickly, several times, then hold the candle by the wick (careful not to burn your fingers!) and dip the other end.

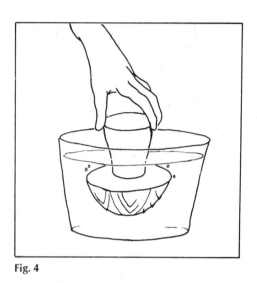

Fig. 4

ASHTRAY MOLDED CANDLE

Ingredients:
Wax: paraffin and stearic acid
Wick: flat- or square-braided
Dye: your choice
Scent: your choice
Ashtray
Knife
Water bath

1. Select an interestingly shaped ashtray, but choose one with a symmetrical design (identical on each side) so that when the two halves of the candle are placed together, the edges will match. Also, make sure that the mouth of the ashtray is wider than the rest of it, so that the candle can slide out.

2. Melt the wax, using the double-boiler method. When it is fully melted, add stearic acid, if not already in the wax (at the rate of 2 tablespoons per pound of wax), and the dye you desire (see page 6 for instructions). Remember that scent oil, if you use it, is the very last thing to add to the wax before pouring (see page 7).

3. Prepare the ashtray by lightly greasing it with cooking oil or silicone mold-release spray.

4. Pour the wax slowly into the ashtray. Let it stand for 30 seconds to let the air bubbles rise.

5. Slowly lower the mold into a water bath, being careful to make sure the water doesn't run over the top of the mold into the wax. Unless you have a highly unusual ashtray, the water bath will not need to be very deep (see figure 1).

6. As the wax cools, a small well will form on the surface. After about 45 minutes,

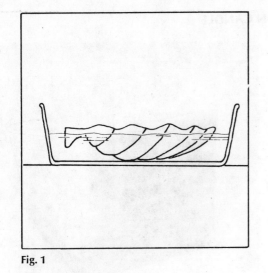

Fig. 1

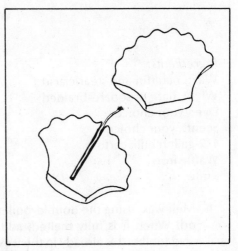

Fig. 2

poke the well with a skewer or knitting needle and refill with hot wax. Do this as often as needed.

7. When the wax has completely hardened, invert the ashtray and drop it gently onto a padded surface to release the wax.

8. Repeat steps 3, 4, 5, 6, and 7 to obtain the other half of your candle. If you have two identical ashtrays, you can ignore this step and save time by making both halves at once.

9. Make sure the 2 halves are level, so that when they are placed together they will fit evenly. If they are not level, scrape them even with a small knife, fill up any small wells with hot wax, or run both flat surfaces over a heated pie pan.

10. Use a scissor point to make a groove down the center of one half, then lay a wax-dipped wick into the groove. Start the wick 1/2 inch from the base and allow 1 inch to protrude beyond the top (see figure 2).

11. Paint the two flat surfaces with hot (230°F) wax of the same color as the rest of the candle and press together, making sure that the edges match up (see figure 3). When the candle has hardened, level off and secure the seams with a heated knife (see figure 4).

12. The candle can be further finished by a quick dip in hot (240°F) wax (see page 10).

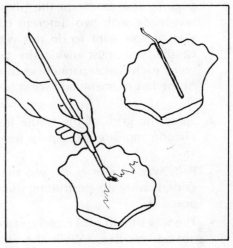

Fig. 3

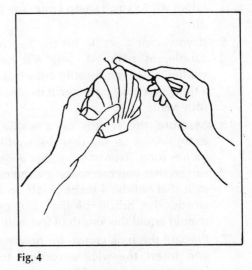

Fig. 4

31

WAFFLE-IRON CANDLE

Ingredients:
Wax: paraffin and stearic acid
Wick: flat- or square-braided
Dye: your choice
Scent: your choice
1/2-gallon milk carton
Waffle iron
Knife

1. Melt wax, using the double-boiler method. When it is fully melted, add stearic acid (unless it is already in the wax) at the rate of 2 tablespoons per pound. Add dye according to the instructions on page 6. The candle in the photograph was made with two different colors of wax; if you want to do this with your candle, you must divide the wax and color each half separately at this point. At the last moment, add scent (see page 7).

2. Spray the grids of the waffle iron with silicone mold-release spray (see figure 1).

3. Pour wax of one color into the waffle grids, leaving the protruding squares exposed.

4. The wax should cool rapidly, since it will not be very deep. While the wax is still somewhat warm, release the waffles from the grids by cutting around the edges with a small sharp knife (see figure 2).

Fig. 1

5. If you want a waffle on the top of the candle, as pictured, you will need 5 waffles. Since most waffle irons make 4 at a time, you must pour again to obtain the fifth waffle.

6. Measure the length of a waffle. For example, let us say that the waffle is 4 inches long. Trim a 1/2-gallon milk carton so that you can make a cube candle in it that will be 4 inches high. In other words, the height of the core candle should equal the length of the waffle.

7. Prepare the milk carton for holding wax and insert the wick according to the instructions on page 10.

Fig. 2

8. Pour wax of the second color, heated to 160°F, slowly into the milk carton (which should be held at a tilt—see figure 3).

9. After about 45 minutes a well or indentation will form around the wick on the surface of the wax; poke 3 holes into the well with a knitting needle and refill the well with hot wax of the same color. Do this as often as the well forms.

10. When the wax has hardened, tear off the carton, and you are ready to start attaching the waffles.

11. There are two possible ways to attach the waffles:

    A. Lay the cube candle on its side, spoon a little hot (240°F) wax of the same color onto the side, and press a waffle in place. Do this for the other three sides as well, taking care that each waffle is firmly secured before you go to the next side.

    B. Heat wax of the same color as the cube to 240°F. Hold the cube candle firmly and dip one side into the hot wax. Then quickly press one of the waffles into place. Continue for the rest of the sides (see figure 4).

12. Heat a barbecue skewer or knitting needle and carefully poke a hole in the center of the fifth waffle. Spoon a little hot wax on the top of the candle, pull the wick through the hole, and press the fifth waffle in place.

13. In order to secure the waffles more firmly to the cube, go over the edges with a wood-burning tool (if you have one) or a heated butter knife.

Fig. 3

Fig. 4

CHAPTER FOUR

ORNATE CANDLES

HAND-DIPPED TAPERS

Ingredients:
Wax: low-melting-point (135°-140° F)
Wick: square-braided
Dye: your choice
Scent: your choice
Metal nut or washer (optional)

1. The ideal container to hold the melted wax for hand-dipped candles would be metal (preferably iron), wide-mouthed, and deeper than the length of the candle you want to make. Unless you plan to make a short taper, it is difficult to find a deep enough container. Although it is not technically the best solution, you can make a taper using an enormous kitchen pot; the kind that is only about 12 inches deep but is very wide-mouthed. Such a container holds about 3 pounds of wax.

2. Melt wax (low-melting-point), using the double-boiler method. Do not add stearic acid. Add the dye of your choice (see page 6). Pour the wax into the dipping container and maintain it at a heat of 155°-160° F.

34

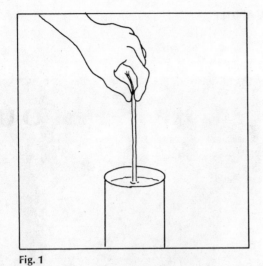

Fig. 1

Fig. 2

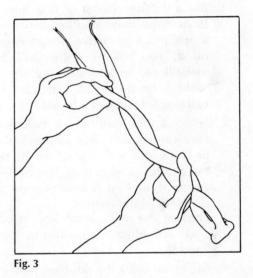

Fig. 3

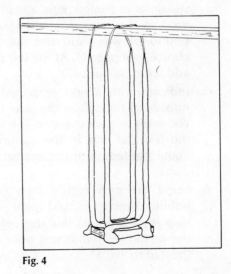

Fig. 4

3. Cut a length of wick about 6 inches longer than the actual length of the candle. This is to allow you enough to hold on to while dipping. If you want a dripless candle, use square-braided wick. If you want a dripping-type candle, choose a flat-braided wick.

4. Optional: tie a small metal nut or washer onto the end of the wick. This serves to weight the end of the taper, making it straighter as it cools. The reason this step is optional is that unless you have the ideal wax container (deep), the metal washer will make it difficult to draw the wick through the wax.

5. Dip the wick for 3 minutes in the melted wax, then smooth it straight between your fingers as it cools. This will help you avoid an uneven surface on the candle.

6. Dip the wick into the hot wax for 2 to 3 seconds, lift it out slowly and let it dry for 2 to 3 minutes (see figure 1).

7. Repeat step 7 until your candle is as thick as you want it (see figure 2).

8. Keep the candle away from drafts as you let it dry, since breezes can affect its shape. The ideal way of cooling is to hang the candle up, but you can speed the process by running cool water over the wax.

9. To make interesting arrangements with hand-dipped tapers, twist and/or knot them into desired shapes (see figures 3 and 4) while they are still warm; then let them cool in the air.

COASTER CANDLE

Ingredients:
Wax: paraffin and stearic acid
Wick: flat- or square-braided
Dye: your choice
Scent: your choice
Milk carton
Coaster or soap dish
Flat-bottomed container to hold 2 inches of
    cold water
Water bath
Antiquing paint (optional)

1. Buy a shallow coaster or soap dish, plastic or metal, that has either an interesting shape or an attractive design engraved on it. You will need to make 5 wax medallions, so you can use the same mold 5 times—unless you want to be extravagant and buy 5 molds.

2. Select a milk carton as a mold for the core candle. Whether you pick a quart or half gallon will depend on the size of the coaster or soap dish. The side of the carton should be *at least* as wide as the diameter of the coaster.

3. Prepare the milk carton and insert the wick according to the instructions on page 10.

4. Melt wax, using the double-boiler method, to 160°F. When it is fully melted, add stearic acid (unless it is already in the wax) at the rate of 2 tablespoons per pound of wax. Add the dye of your choice (see page 6). At the last moment, add scent (see page 7).

5. Indicate with a pen or pencil on the outside of the carton the level to which you want to pour the wax. The height of the level of wax in the carton should equal the length of the coaster or soap dish.

6. Stand the milk carton in a container holding 2 inches of cold water. This is to stop any seam leaks that may form. Hold the carton at a tilt as you pour the wax (heated to 160°F).

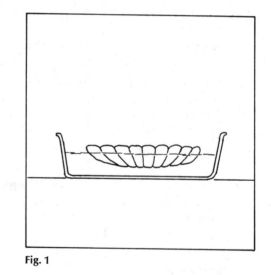

Fig. 1

7. Melt wax for the coaster, using the double-boiler method. Add stearic acid, dye, and finally scent as in step 4.

8. Lightly grease the coaster with cooking oil or silicone mold-release spray.

9. With metal coasters, pour the wax at 190°F. Soap dishes, on the other hand, are generally plastic, so with these don't pour wax above 160°F.

10. Float the coaster in a shallow pan of cold

water to let the wax harden (see figure 1). Don't let the water get into the liquid wax. When the wax solidifies, pop it out.

11. Make a total of 5 wax medallions from the coaster or soap dish.

12. When the wax in the carton has hardened, tear off the paper (see figure 2).

13. Use a nail or scissor point to make score marks on the sides of the core candle and on the backs of the wax medallions. This is to aid in making the medallions adhere to the core candle.

14. Brush a side of the candle and the back of a wax medallion with 240°F wax and press them together (see figure 3). Hold pressed together until the wax hardens. Repeat this step for the other 3 sides.

15. Trim the fifth medallion so that it will fit on top of the candle. Using a heated skewer (be careful not to burn your fingers), poke a hole for the wick through the medallion. Thread wick through hole and fasten this piece to the top of the candle, using the procedure in step 14.

16. Heat the blade of a butter knife and pass it lightly over the edges of the medallions to blend them into the body of the candle.

17. A final touch can be added by rubbing the candle with antiquing paint, such as Rub 'n Buff.

Fig. 2

Fig. 3

CARVED CLAY CANDLE

Ingredients:
Wax: paraffin and stearic acid
Wick: flat- or square-braided, wick tab
Dye: your choice
Scent: your choice
Mylar vinyl
Water-base clay
Small sharp knife
Carving tool (optional)
Masking tape
Sandbox (optional)
Antiquing paint (optional)

1. Buy a piece of Mylar, a very flexible vinyl, and cut it to at least 8 inches in length and 10 inches in height. The length of the vinyl will be 1 inch more than the circumference of your candle. For example, a piece of vinyl 8 inches long will make a candle with a 7-inch circumference.

2. Knead water-base clay until it is flexible, and smooth it evenly onto the vinyl, making it 1/4-inch thick throughout (see figure 1).

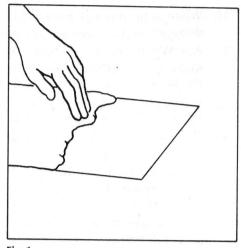

Fig. 1

3. Using a knife or a carving tool, carve a design into the clay. Floral, abstract, and geometric designs work out well (see figure 2).

4. Cut 1 inch of clay away from 1 of the 8-inch edges of the vinyl. This is to allow for an overlap when you roll it up.

5. Roll up the vinyl, clay side inside, so that the clay edges meet inside the tube and the 1 inch of uncovered vinyl overlaps on the outside. Tape the edges securely together with masking tape on the outside.

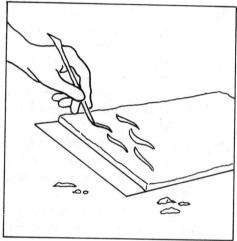

Fig. 2

6. With a stick or your finger (if the mold is wide enough) go over the clay seam on the inside and smooth the edges together.

7. There are two methods of supporting the mold: the first is make a base for the tube mold by preparing a large disc of clay, then pressing the tube down into it. The second is stand the tube in a box and pack damp sand firmly around it.

8. Use a weighted wick (see page 8) and suspend it in the mold from a pencil centered across the top (see figure 3).

9. Melt the wax, using the double-boiler method. When it is fully melted, add stearic acid (unless it is already in the wax) at the rate of 2 tablespoons per pound of wax. Add the dye of your choice according to the instructions on page 6, and at the last moment add the scent (see page 7).

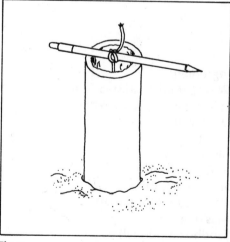

Fig. 3

10. When the wax is 180°F, pour it slowly down the side of the mold.

11. After about 45 minutes, a well will form in the surface of the candle. Puncture the surface 3 times with a knitting needle or a pencil and refill well with hot wax. Do this as often as the well forms.

12. When the wax has completely hardened, untape the mold and remove it. If clay clings, run the candle under water (see figure 4).

13. Antiquing paint, such as Rub 'n Buff, can be used to give a nice finish to a carved-clay candle.

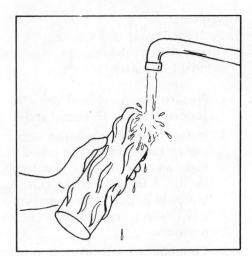

Fig. 4

VARIATIONS ON CARVED CLAY CANDLE

Ingredients:
Same as for Carved-Clay Candle
Small pieces of colored glass

1. Prepare the vinyl and the clay as explained on page 38, steps 1 and 2.

2. Break pieces of colored glass into small, irregular shapes. You may be able to buy such pieces of glass at a craft store.

3. Place the pieces of glass on the clay. See illustration.

4. Take a tiny amount of clay and barely cover the bottom edge of each piece of glass. This will hold the glass on the clay so that it won't fall off when you lift up the vinyl, but it will not keep the glass from sticking to the wax once it is poured.

5. Carefully roll the vinyl into a cylinder, taping the outside edges together with masking tape.

6. Continue with steps 6 through 12 on pages 38 and 39.

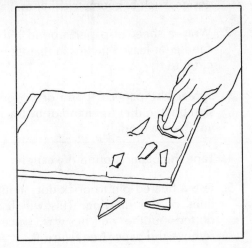

Ingredients:
Same as for Carved-Clay Candle
An object with a raised design: glass, carved
    pendant, or button

1. Prepare the vinyl and the clay as explained on page 38, steps 1 and 2.

2. Instead of carving a design into the clay, use an object that has a raised design to make an imprint. A cut-glass tumbler can be rolled firmly over the clay. A carved button or pendant can be pressed into the clay, with space left between the impressions.

3. Continue with steps 4 through 13 on pages 38 and 39.

ETCHED CANDLE

Ingredients:
Tubular candle (approximately 3-inch diameter)
Thin sheet of paper
Masking tape
Sewing pin
Carving tool or sharp knife

1. Decide upon a design that pleases you. You can choose a single-unit pattern, such as a flower or a face, or an allover design, such as geometric shapes.

2. Wrap a sheet of paper around a tubular candle (at least 3 inches in diameter) and cut it to fit.

3. Spread the paper flat and draw your design on it, either freehand or by tracing (if you have a model).

4. Tape the paper around the candle.

5. Use a heated pin to prick dots along the lines of the drawing. This will leave a dotted outline on the wax, once you remove the paper (see figure 1).

Fig. 1

6. You can use a sharp knife as a carving tool, but a V-shaped grooving instrument, such as a wood carver, will yield better results. Gouge out the wax along the guide lines, applying moderate pressure (see figure 2).

7. If you find, once you have finished, that your candle has rough edges, run it quickly under hot water to smooth the messy spots.

8. To decorate further, paint the grooves with colored wax, using a small brush. See Chapter VII for painting techniques.

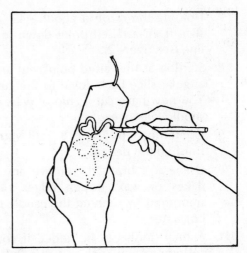

Fig. 2

CHIP-CARVED CANDLE

Ingredients:
Tubular candle (approximately 3-inch diameter)
Tracing paper
Masking tape
Ballpoint pen
Ruler
Single-edged razor blade
Soft brush
Antiquing paint (optional)

1. Select a tubular candle (about 3 inches in diameter) and wrap tracing paper around it, cutting paper to fit.

2. Remove the paper, lay it flat, and trace the design from figure 1 onto it.

3. Tape the paper around the candle. Using a ballpoint pen and a ruler, trace over the design.

4. Remove the tracing paper and you will have on the candle a clear outline of the design.

5. Using a single-edged razor blade, cut around the *outside* lines of the pattern.

6. The lines running from the center out to the points of the design indicate where the raised portions of the pattern will be. The dotted lines running from the center to the indented parts of the pattern show where the indentations will be. Make a deep cut with the razor along the dotted indentation lines.

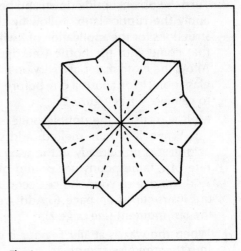

Fig. 1

41

7. Holding the razor at about a 45° angle, slice from a raised point down to a cut line (see figure 2).

8. Starting at the raised point, cut another angular slice back down to the cut line. You now have cut a chip of wax, which should fall out easily.

9. Continue steps 7 and 8 until you have finished the design.

10. Use a soft brush to remove any loose flakes of wax. Rough edges can be smoothed by running the candle under hot water.

11. A final finish can be added if you rub antiquing paint, such as Rub 'n Buff, over the design.

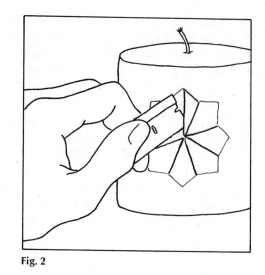

Fig. 2

CUT-GLASS CANDLE*

Ingredients:
Wax: paraffin and stearic acid
Wick: wire-core
Dye: your choice
Scent: your choice
Kwikmold
Cut-glass object

* W. Spencer, Inc., Portland, Maine

1. The candle in the photograph was made from a cut-glass vase and Kwikmold, a new liquid rubber latex distributed by W. Spencer, Inc., Portland, Maine. Other cut-glass items that work well as candle forms are candlesticks, tumblers, bowls, and cups.

2. Turn the object upside down and begin to apply the rubber latex, following the instructions for the application of Kwikmold that come with the bottle (see figure 1). Allow the mold material to dry on the cut-glass object for about a day before trying to remove it (see figure 2).

3. Melt wax, using the double-boiler method. When it is fully melted, add stearic acid (if it is not already in the wax) at the rate of 2 tablespoons per pound of wax. Add the dye of your choice according to the instructions on page 6. Add scent at the last moment (see page 7).

4. When the wax is at 180°F, pour it slowly into the mold (see figure 3).

Fig. 1

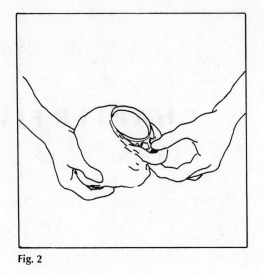

Fig. 2

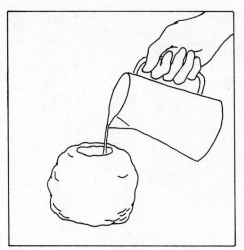

Fig. 3

5. About 45 minutes after pouring, the cooling wax will develop a well or indentation on its surface. Poke 3 holes in the well, using a knitting needle or pencil. Insert a wire-core wick, then refill with hot wax, taking care that the wick remains straight. Refer to step 15, on page 104 (Beachcomber Candle), for a variation.

6. When the wax has fully hardened, peel back the rubber mold (which can, of course, be used over and over again).

7. The candle in the photograph was decorated as follows: several different colored waxes were brushed onto the candle in a vertical direction (see figure 4). A butane torch was then used to glaze the colors to the candle. A dip in hot (240°F) clear wax (see page 10), then in room-temperature water add the final touch.

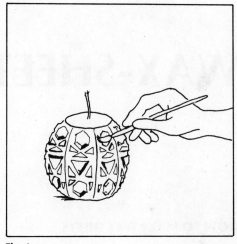

Fig. 4

CHAPTER FIVE

WAX-SHEET CANDLES

HOW TO MAKE WAX SHEETS

Ingredients:
Wax: low-melting-point (130°-135° F) paraffin
Dye: your choice
Cooking oil or silicone mold-release spray
Cookie sheet or cake pan

1. You will need a rectangular cake pan or a cookie sheet with a rim in order to make the wax sheets.

2. Use wax with a low (130°-135° F) melting point. You might have difficulty in getting enough flexibility in the wax sheets when you use straight paraffin wax. W. Spencer, Inc., a candle company that makes many wax-sheet candles, recommends a mix of 1 cup of beeswax to 2 quarts of 133° F paraffin.

3. Melt wax, using the double-boiler method, to 170° F. Do not add stearic acid. Add the dye according to the instructions on page 6.

4. Lightly grease the pan or tray with cooking oil or silicone mold-release spray.

5. Slowly pour a thin (1/4-inch) layer of wax onto the pan.

6. Let the wax cool slowly until you cannot easily dent it with a fingertip. The wax should still be pliable.

7. Use a sharp knife to cut around the edge of the pan and lift the wax sheet out.

8. Repeat this procedure to make as many wax sheets as you need for your candle.

9. If the wax sheets become too rigid and stiff to be easily bent, soften them in one of three ways: a) immerse them in warm water; b) hold them in steam; or c) put them on wax paper on top of a heating pad.

44

EDGED CANDLE

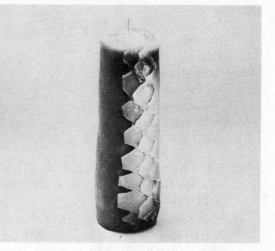

Ingredients:
Wax: low-melting-point (130°-135° F)
    paraffin
    beeswax (optional)
Wick: flat- or square-braided
Dye: 3 colors
Scent: your choice
3 cookie sheets
Small sharp knife

1. Melt wax (see step 2, page 44), using the double-boiler method, to 170° F. Do not add stearic acid.

2. Divide the wax into 3 containers and add a different color dye to each. Add the scent at the last moment (see page 7).

3. Pour 3 different wax sheets, each in a different color (see page 44).

4. Cut the wick so that it is 2 inches longer than the width of the sheets. Dip the wick in hot wax and straighten it between your fingers. Let it harden.

5. Allow the sheets to cool to the point where you can't easily dent them with a fingertip. Cut around the edges of the cookie sheets with a sharp knife and lift the sheets out.

6. Lay the 3 sheets on top of each other, making sure they are the same size and that the edges line up. If not, trim them with a knife.

7. Place the wick at one end of the stacked sheets.

8. Making sure that the sheets remain pliable, roll the edge of the sheets over the wick and continue rolling until you have a tubular candle. As you roll, take care that the edges remain in line (see figure 1).

9. Take a small sharp knife and cut decorative edges for each color, making sure each color is exposed (see figure 2).

10. Let the candle cool thoroughly. Lay the candle on its side and shift its position while cooling to maintain the tube shape. Trim any uneven edges when fully cooled.

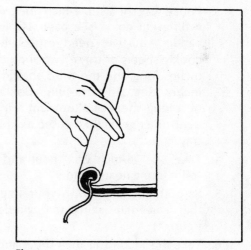

Fig. 1

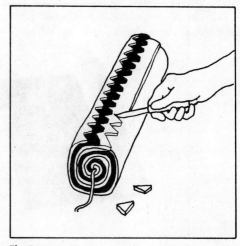

Fig. 2

ROLLED TUBE CANDLE

Ingredients:
Wax: low-melting-point (130°-135°F)
      paraffin
      beeswax (optional)
Wick: wire-core
Dye: 3 colors
Scent: your choice
3 cookie sheets
Large sharp knife

1. Melt wax (see step 2, page 44), using the double-boiler method, to 170°F. Do not add stearic acid.

2. Divide the wax into 3 containers and add a different color dye to each. Pick colors that blend well. Add scent at the last minute (see page 7).

3. Pour 3 wax sheets, 1/4-inch thick, each in a different color (see page 44). For this candle you will need especially long cookie sheets or trays. Two should be 16 inches long and the third should be 24 inches long. An extra-long cookie sheet or a long sheet of aluminum foil with a bent-up edge could be used as a pouring tray.

4. Take one 16-inch wax sheet and firmly roll it into a neat cylinder.

5. Smooth the edge with your fingers so that it lies flat against the cylinder (see figure 1).

6. Take the second 16-inch sheet and press one edge firmly against the cylinder, so

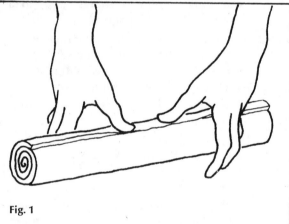

Fig. 1

Fig. 2

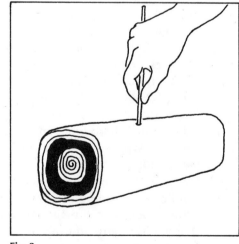

Fig. 3

46

that it fits tightly. Rolling in the opposite direction (see figure 2), wind the second sheet around the first cylinder. Press the loose edge flat against the rolled wax.

7. Press the edge of the final sheet of wax, the longest one, against what you've already made. Continue with step 6.

8. Let the wax cool, shifting its position as necessary to maintain the tubular shape.

9. Using a heated skewer (see page 10), make a wick hole and insert a wire-core wick in the side of the tube (see figure 3).

10. Slightly heat a very sharp knife and cut off 2 wedges, one at each end of the tube (see figure 4).

11. Dip the candle into a hot (240°F) clear wax bath in order to smooth the edges (see page 10).

12. You can decorate this candle by painting

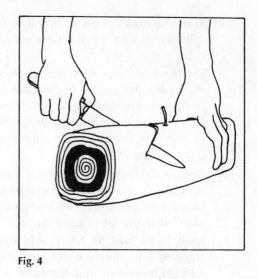

Fig. 4

wax on the surface. See Chapter VII for the technique.

COILED CUBE CANDLE

Ingredients:
Wax: low-melting-point (130°-135°F) para-paraffin
    beeswax (optional)
Wick: wire-core
Dye: 4 colors
Scent: your choice
4 cookie sheets
1/2-gallon milk carton
Water-base clay
Sharp knife

1. Prepare the 1/2-gallon milk carton for a mold according to the instructions on page 15.

2. Melt wax, using the double-boiler method, to 170°F. Do not add stearic acid.

3. Divide the wax into 4 containers and add a different color dye to each. Add scent at last moment (see page 7).

4. Pour 4 wax sheets, each in a different color (see page 44). The sheets do not need to be very large; approximately 8-inch square is suitable.

5. When the wax has cooled to the point where you can't easily dent it with a fingertip, with a sharp knife cut thin strips (1/2-inch wide) from the different colors.

6. Select a strip and roll it up tightly.

7. Take a strip of a different color and roll it around the first. Make sure the ends are pressed smooth and the edges align (very important! — see figure 1).

8. The roll you are making should eventually fit against one of the inside walls of the milk carton mold, with 1/2-inch to spare on either side. Keep adding strips to the roll until it becomes the correct size.

9. While the wax is still warm and pliable, make 4 more rolls for the other sides and the top of the candle.

47

10. Trim the milk carton so that its height is 1/2 inch more than the diameter of your rolls.

11. Lay the carton on its side and place one roll inside the carton, against the middle of the bottom side. Again, it is important that the roll fit smoothly against the wall of the carton, so make sure that the edges of the roll are even.

12. Press water-base clay around the edge of the carton, building a kind of dam so that when you pour wax into the carton it won't leak out (see figure 2).

13. Melt more wax to 180°F, add dye (see page 6) and finally scent (see page 7), and pour wax around the roll—about a 1/2-inch layer.

14. Let this side harden before shifting the carton to another side. Continue with steps 11 through 13 for the other 3 sides.

15. Fill the inside of the candle with more 180°F wax, of the same color as you've been pouring around the rolls.
Rest the 5th roll on the top and add wax around it until the level of the wax and the roll are the same.

16. Let the candle harden completely. Tear off the milk carton.

17. Use a heated skewer to make a wick hole, then insert the wick (see page 10).

18. If wax has run over the edge of a roll, scrape it off with a single-edged razor blade.

Fig. 1

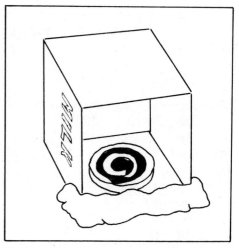
Fig. 2

COOKIE-CUTTER LAYERED CANDLE

Ingredients:
Wax: low-melting-point (130°-135°F) paraffin
Wick: flat- or square-braided
Dye: 2 colors
Scent: your choice
Round cookie cutter
2 cookie sheets
Sharp knife

1. Melt the wax, using the double-boiler method, to 170°F. Do not add stearic acid.

2. Divide the wax into 2 containers and add a different color dye to each; finally add scent (see page 7).

48

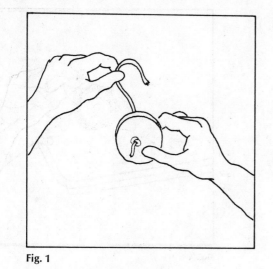

Fig. 1

Fig. 2

3. Pour 2 wax sheets, each a different color (see page 44).

4. Use a round cookie cutter to cut circles from each sheet.

5. Punch a hole with a skewer in the center of one of the wax circles. Thread the wick through it and tie the end into a tight knot (or use a wick tab, page 9—see figure 1).

6. Punch a hole in a second circle, and continue to stack the circles tightly on the wick, alternating the colors. Make sure the edges line up (see figure 2).

7. Let the candle harden.

8. Use a sharp knife to even off any edges that stick out (see figure 3).

9. A quick dip in a hot (240°F) clear wax bath will add a smoother finish to the candle,

Fig. 3

as well as hold the circles together more securely (see page 10).

MUSHROOM CANDLE*

Ingredients:
Wax: paraffin with a 133°F melting point
      beeswax
Wick: flat-braided
Dye: your choice, powdered
Scent: your choice
Cookie sheet
Sharp knife
Large glass or round cookie cutter
Small jars
Butane torch

1. Using a mixture of 1/2 cup beeswax to 1 quart of 133°F-melting-point paraffin, melt the wax to 170°F. It is not necessary

* W. Spencer, Inc., Portland, Maine

Fig. 1

Fig. 2

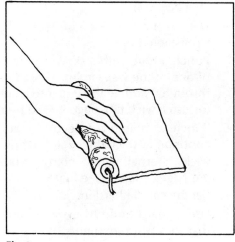

Fig. 3

to add dye; certainly don't add stearic acid, since it would make the wax less manageable. Speed is important in making this candle, so that the wax remains pliable.

2. Put different-colored powdered dyes in separate small jars. These jars should have a hole in the center of their lids, punched with an ice pick or drilled, so that they can serve as shakers.

3. Pour a 1/2-inch layer of wax into the cookie sheet (see page 44).

4. After 3 minutes, scatter-sprinkle the different-color dyes onto the wax (see figure 1).

5. Use a butane torch to go quickly over the top of the wax so that the powdered dye melts and glazes (see figure 2).

6. Wait 3 to 5 minutes. Using a sharp knife, cut a 4- by 4-inch square of wax and lift it out of the cookie sheet onto a flat surface, colored side down.

7. Lay the wick along one edge of the square, with 3 inches of wick sticking out. Roll it up (see figure 3).

8. Mold and press the wax with your fingers to make the mushroom stem. Flatten the bottom of the roll into a base by pressing it against the table (see figure 4).

9. Use a sharp knife, a large glass, or a cookie cutter to make a wax circle 5 inches in diameter. Lift it out of the cookie sheet.

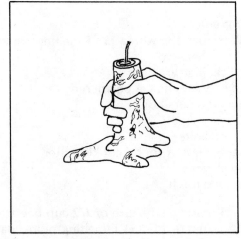

Fig. 4

10. Poke a hole through the center of the circle and thread the wick through. Bend the circle into an appropriate mushroom cap shape, as illustrated in figure 5.

11. To add a charming touch, purchase tiny plastic animals from the five-and-ten and position them by firmly pressing them into the wax base.

12. Dip the mushroom in a hot (240°F) wax bath as follows: First, holding the candle by the base, dip the cap and the top of the stem. This will seal the two together. Then, holding it by the wick, dip the whole candle (see page 10).

13. A quick dunk in room-temperature water will add gloss.

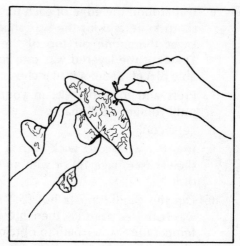

Fig. 5

HAND-ROLLED CANDLE*

* W. Spencer, Inc., Portland, Maine

Ingredients:
Wax: paraffin with a 133°F melting point
        beeswax
Wick: wire-core
Dye: your choice, and powdered black
Scent: your choice
2 cookie sheets
Sharp knife
Wax bath

1. Use a wax mixture with a ratio of 1/2 cup beeswax to 1 quart of 133°F-melting-point paraffin. Melt the wax, using the double-boiler method, to 170°F. Do not add stearic acid.

2. When the wax is fully melted, pour half into another container and add the dye of your choice to that half (see page 6).

3. Pour 2 1/2-inch-deep wax sheets, one clear wax (see figure 1), the other dyed.

4. After 3 minutes, shake powdered black dye evenly over the surface of one of the sheets. (See page 50 for instructions on making the shaker.) Then torch the surface with a butane torch until the black dye melts and glazes (see figure 2).

5. Let the wax in each tray cool until it cannot be easily dented with fingertip pressure.

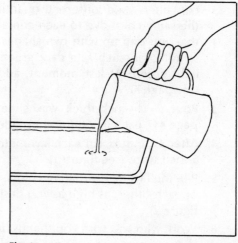

Fig. 1

51

6. Cut around the edge of each tray with a sharp knife and lift the wax sheets out. Layer them one on top of the other. Then cut the layered wax into manageable pieces, about 4 by 8 inches.

7. Press and fold the wax in your hands until you get a ball shape.

8. Let it cool.

9. Insert a wire-core wick with a heated skewer (see page 10) or with an electric drill.

10. Dip the candle into a hot (240°F) clear wax bath (see page 10), then into a room-temperature water bath to obtain a high gloss.

Fig. 2

MARBELIZED CANDLE

Ingredients:
Wax: low-melting-point (130°-135°F)
         paraffin
         beeswax (optional)
Wick: wire-core
Dye: your choice
Scent: your choice
2 cookie sheets
Sharp knife
Wax bath

1. Melt wax (see step 2, page 44), using the double-boiler method, to 170°F. Do not add stearic acid.

2. Pour half of the liquid wax into another container. Add different quantities of the same color dye to each container so that you end up with two shades of the same color, such as a dark green and a light green. At last moment, add scent (see page 7).

3. Pour 2 1/4-inch-thick wax sheets (see page 44), each in a different shade.

4. After 3 minutes, cut each layer into 2- by 6-inch strips (see figure 1).

5. Pile the layers, alternating colors, on top of each other, as high as you desire (see figure 2).

6. Work with wax with your hands until the layers merge and you get a marbelized

Fig. 1

52

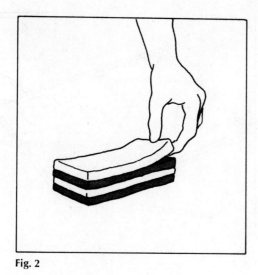

Fig. 2

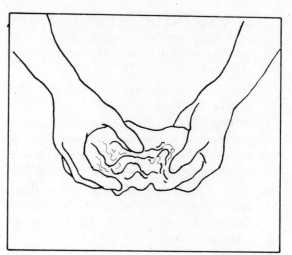

Fig. 3

effect (see figure 3).

7. Tightly press the wax into a roughly cube-shaped mass.

8. After the wax has cooled, take a heated sharp knife and cut the mass at the edges, making a cube or an oblong (see figure 4).

9. Insert the wick with a heated barbecue skewer (see page 10).

10. After the wick has hardened in place, dip the candle into a hot (240°F) clear wax bath to smooth any rough edges (see page 10).

Fig. 4

ROLLED STROBE*

Ingredients:

Wax: paraffin with a 133°F melting point
      beeswax

Wick: 2 dowel sticks, 12 inches long, 3/16-inch diameter

Dye: your choice, powdered

Scent: your choice

Cookie sheet or baking pan, 6 x 26 inches

Sharp knife

Wax bath

1. Using a mixture with the ratio of 1/2 cup beeswax to 1 quart of 133°F-melting-point wax, melt the wax to 170°F, using the

* W. Spencer, Inc., Portland, Maine

53

double-boiler method. Do not add stearic acid. Add dye according to the instructions on page 6, and at the last moment add scent (see page 7).

2. Pour a 1/4-inch layer of wax into the cookie sheet (see page 44).

3. After 3 minutes, shake powdered dye (see the method for making a shaker on page 50) over the surface of the wax. Use a butane torch to glaze the colors together.

4. After 4 more minutes, cut with a sharp knife around the edge of the tray to release the wax, which should still be warm and pliable.

5. Make a diagonal cut from one corner to the opposite corner, creating 2 right-angled triangles. Each triangle will make a separate candle (see figure 1).

6. Place one of the triangles, dyed side down, on a clean flat surface.

7. Lay a dowel stick (12 by 3/16 inches) along the edge, as pictured in figure 2, and press the wax edge firmly against it. Roll the wax evenly around the dowel stick and press the edge neatly against the rolled wax.

8. Dip the strobe several times in a hot (240° F) clear wax bath so that you obtain a clear wax coating (see page 10). A quick dip in room-temperature water will complete the candle.

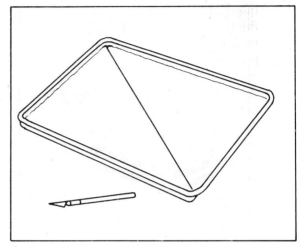

Fig. 1

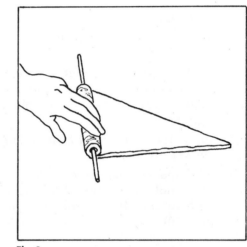

Fig. 2

ROLLED STROBE WITH PETALS

Ingredients:
Wax: paraffin with a 133° F melting point
    beeswax
Wick: dowel stick, 12 inches long, 3/16-inch
    diameter
Dye: your choice
Scent: your choice
Cookie sheet, 8 x 10 inches
Sharp knife
Wax bath

1. The wax for this candle should be a mix with the ratio of 1/2 cup beeswax to 1

quart of 133° F-melting-point wax. Using the double-boiler method, melt the wax to 170° F. Do not add stearic acid.

2. Pour half of the wax into a separate container. Following the instructions for dye on page 6, add dye to this container. Leave the other half of the wax clear. Add scent at last moment to each container of wax (see page 7).

3. Pour a 1/8-inch-deep layer of clear wax into the cookie sheet (see page 44). This will dry white.

4. Wait 1 minute, then prop up one end of the pan with a pencil or slender book. This will result in a wax sheet that is thicker at one end than at the other.

5. When the wax sheet has cooled so that it doesn't dent easily from fingertip pressure, pour the dyed wax in a 1/8-inch-deep layer over the white wax (see figure 1). The pan should still be propped up.

6. Let the wax cool to the point where it passes the fingertip-dent test. Cut around the edge of the cookie sheet with a sharp knife and lift the wax out onto a clean flat surface.

7. Place the dowel stick along the long side of the wax sheet.

8. Start rolling the wax around the stick (see figure 2). You will find that it rolls at an angle because of the uneven thickness.

9. When the wax is all rolled up, press the edges smooth.

10. Using a sharp knife, carefully cut the uneven wax away at the top of the candle.

11. To create the petal look, make slanting cuts into the wax with the knife (see figure 3).

12. Then *gently* pull the wax out into the petals at the places where you've made cuts.

13. Dip the candle quickly in and out of hot (240° F) clear wax to smooth the rough spots and add finish (see page 10).

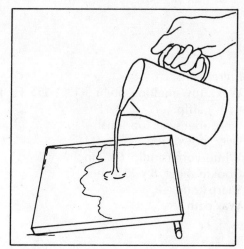

Fig. 1

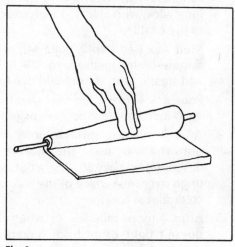

Fig. 2

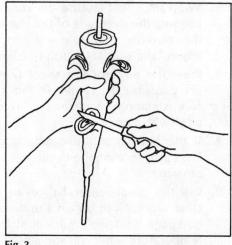

Fig. 3

55

WRAPPED CANDLE*

Ingredients:
Wax: low-melting-point (130°-135°F) par-
     affin
     beeswax (optional)
Dye: powdered
White-core candle, 6 x 2 inches
Cookie sheet, 8 x 20 inches
Sharp knife
Wax bath

* W. Spencer, Inc., Portland, Maine

1. A 6-inch-tall and 2-inch-diameter white candle is used as a core for the wrapped candle. Try to select a core candle with a long wick, with at least 1 inch sticking out of the candle.

2. Melt wax (see step 2, page 44), using the double-boiler method, to 170°F. Do not add stearic acid. Do not add dye or scent.

3. Pour a 1/4-inch-deep wax sheet in a 20-by 8-inch cookie sheet (see page 44).

4. After 3 minutes, sprinkle powdered dye onto the wax, using the shaker method described on page 50. Use a butane torch to go over the surface of the wax until the color glazes together.

5. After 3 more minutes, or when the wax doesn't dent easily from fingertip pressure, cut with a sharp knife around the edges of the sheet and lift it out (see figure 1).

Fig. 1

6. Wrap the sheet around the core candle, keeping the dyed side of the wax sheet to the outside, and fold the ends over around the wick at the top (see figure 2).

7. Press the edge of the sheet firmly into place against the candle so that the surface is smooth. If necessary, trim rough edge with a knife.

8. If the bottom of the candle is uneven, level it by rotating the candle on a heated pie pan.

9. Dip the candle several times in a 240°F clear wax bath to obtain a uniform finish (see page 10). Then a quick dunk in room-temperature water will add gloss.

Fig. 2

56

Ingredients:
Wax: paraffin with a 133°F melting point
      beeswax (optional)
Wick: wire-core
Dye: your choice
Scent: your choice
Cookie sheet
Small bowl or custard cup
Sharp knife
Paper cup
Wax bath

1. Melt wax (see step 2, page 44), using the double-boiler method, to 170°F. Do not add stearic acid. Add the dye of your choice (see page 6). If you want the center of your flower to be a different color, reserve the wax for it at this point. At the last moment, add scent (see page 7).

2. Pour a 1/8-inch-deep wax sheet according to the instructions on page 44.

3. Let the wax cool until you can't dent it easily with a fingertip. It should, however, still be warm and pliable.

4. Use a small sharp knife to cut petal shapes in the wax. You will need 10 petals altogether: 4 large ones for the outside of the flower, 3 medium, and 3 small ones (see figure 1).

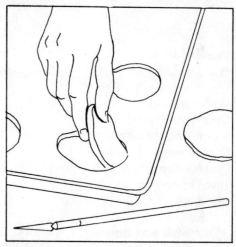

Fig. 1

5. Place the 4 large petals in a small shallow bowl or custard cup and arrange them so that they overlap. Gently bend the tip of each petal so that it curves outward (see figure 2).

6. Pour a small pool (1/4 inch deep) of liquid wax, the same color as the petals, into the bottom of the bowl. This will hold the petals together, as well as form a base for the candle.

7. Place the 3 medium petals inside the first 4 and overlap their edges as well.

8. Repeat step 7 with the last 3 petals.

9. When the petals are cold, fill the center

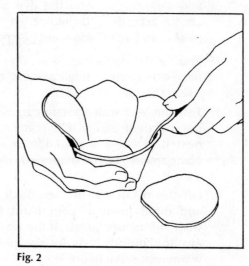

Fig. 2

of the flower with hot wax. Since the center is so small, use a paper cup with a bent rim as a pouring pitcher (see figure 3).

10. When a crust forms, insert a short wick. It is unlikely that a well will form on the surface of the cooling wax, since the mold is so small. If it does, however, poke 3 holes with a knitting needle or pencil and refill with hot wax.

11. Dip the candle into hot (240°F) clear wax (see page 10), then into room-temperature water, to add gloss.

12. You can replace the center, once it has burned down, with more hot wax or with a votive candle.

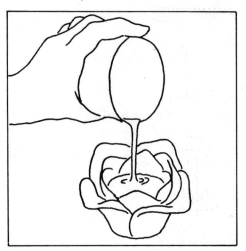

Fig. 3

FLOWER CANDLE II

Ingredients:
Wax: paraffin with a 133°F melting point
      beeswax (optional)
Wick: wire-core
Dye: your choice
Scent: your choice
Cookie sheet
Custard cup
Sharp knife
Wax bath

1. Melt wax (see step 2, page 44), using the double-boiler method, to 170°F. Do not add stearic acid. Add the dye of your choice according to the instructions on page 6, and finally add scent (see page 7).

2. Pour a 1/8-inch-deep wax sheet (see page 44). Leave a small amount of wax still in the pot.

3. Test the wax with your finger; when it doesn't dent easily, it is ready for the next step. Use a sharp knife or a razor blade to cut 11 petal shapes—8 large and 3 small.

4. Lift the petals out of the cookie sheet and mold them in your hand to the shape of realistic petals. If the wax hardens too quickly, handle the petals in warm water (see figure 1).

5. Place 4 petals in a custard cup so that the edges lightly overlap.

6. Heat the wax left in the pot and add it to the center of the custard cup, forming a small pool to hold the petals in place (see figure 2).

7. Carefully place the next 4 petals in the cup, making sure they are immersed at the base in the pool of hot wax (see

58

1. Beachcomber candle, *page 103* 2. Waffle-iron candle, *page 32*
3. Decoupage candle, *page 85* 4. Marbelized candle, *page 52* 5. Mood
candle, *page 114* 6. Easter egg candle, *page 69.*

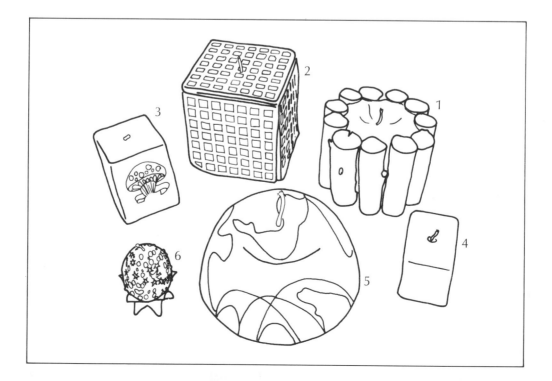

1. Free-form candle, *page 101* 2. Acrylic-painted candle, *page 82*
3. Wax-dripped candle, *page 79* 4. Autumn tomato candle, *page 70* 5. Ice-cream-soda candle, *page 76* 6. Easter egg candle, *page 69*.

1. Two-wick cardboard-box candle, *page 20* 2. Edged candle, *page 45*
3. Wax-painted candle, *page 78* 4. Flower candle II, *page 58* 5. Triangle sand candle, *page 100*.

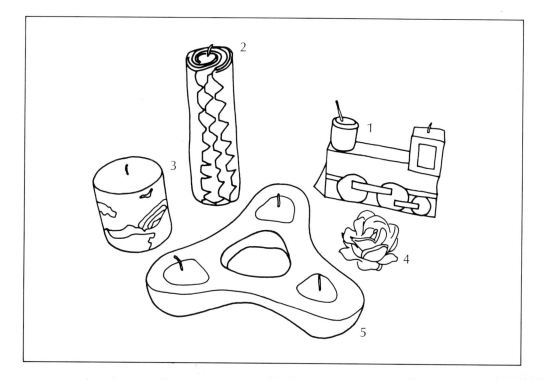

1. Driftwood candle, *page 106* 2. Swirl-painted candle, *page 81*
3. Cooky-cutter layered candle, *page 48* 4. Corrugated candle, *page 18*
5. Layered chunk candle, *page 93*.

1. Chunk candle, *page 92* 2. Cut-glass candle, *page 42* 3. Free-form
clay-cast candle, *page 109* 4. Aluminum-foil free-form candle, *page 22*
5. Concentric-colors candle, *page 90* 6. Flower candle I, *page 57*
7. Layered candle, *page 88*.

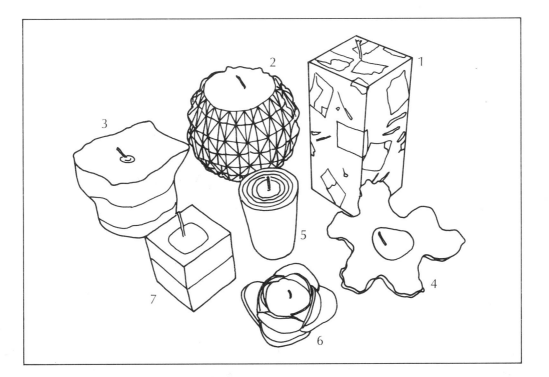

1. Water candle, *page 116* 2. Coiled cube candle, *page 47* 3. Variation on carved clay candle, *page 39* 4. Wrapped candle, *page 56* 5. Hand-rolled candle, *page 51* 6. Rolled tube candle, *page 46*.

1. Ice-cube candle, *page 95* 2. Sponge-painted candle, *page 81* 3. Plastic-flower candle, *page 86* 4. Ashtray molded candle, *page 30* 5. Layered candle, *page 88* 6. Wax-dripped candle, *page 79* 7. Fourth-of-July strobe, *page 77.*

1. Gelatin-mold mushroom, *page 28* 2. Shell candle, *page 117*
3. Appliqué candle, *page 84* 4. Valentine heart, *page 68* 5. Mushroom
candle, *page 49* 6. Sand candle, *page 96*.

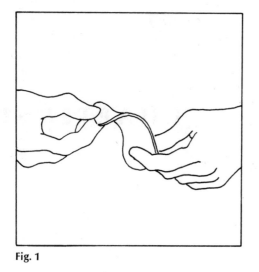
Fig. 1

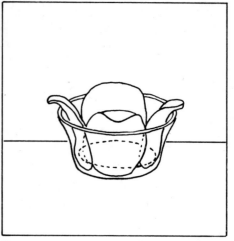
Fig. 2

figure 3). Be very careful not to burn your fingers.

8. Fold 1 of the small petals firmly around a 3-inch wick to form a core. Then wrap the other 2 petals around this core, creating the inner bud of the flower (see figure 4).

9. Carefully insert the petal-wrapped wick into the center of the flower, making certain that it is firmly implanted in the wax pool.

10. When the petals have hardened completely, dip the flower quickly into 200° F clear wax, creating a clear wax film that will hold the petals in place (see page 10).

Fig. 3

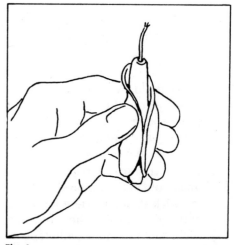
Fig. 4

CHAPTER SIX

CANDLES FOR SPECIAL OCCASIONS

BIRTHDAY CLOWN

Ingredients:
Wax: paraffin and stearic acid
Wick: flat- or square-braided
Dye: red
Scent: your choice
Cone-shaped mold
Masking tape
Tall glass tumbler
Sandbox

1. The cone-shaped candle needed for your clown can be made in either a store-bought mold or a cone-shaped paper cup. You can make your own cone paper mold by cutting a half circle (see figure 1) from heavy paper. Roll it into a cone shape and tape the edges *very* tightly with masking tape. Don't stint on tape—wrap it totally.

2. When you use a paper mold, poke a small hole in the pointed end and thread the wick through. Tie a knot in the end of the wick outside the mold. Secure the wick and the hole with tape to avoid leaks.

3. Pull the wick tight and wrap the loose end around a pencil centered across the top of the cup.

4. Place the cone mold in a tall glass and fill

the glass with cold water so that any leaking wax will harden immediately. Be careful to keep water out of mold. Or, if you have a sandbox at hand, stand the cone upright, wedged in the sand.

5. Melt the wax, using the double-boiler method, to 170° F. When it is fully melted, add stearic acid (if it is not already in the wax) at the rate of 2 tablespoons per pound of wax.

6. Pour half of the wax into a separate container and add a small amount of red dye (see page 6), so that the wax becomes pink. Add scent to both containers at the last moment (see page 7).

7. Pour the pink wax into the bottom half of the cone. Let it harden so that a crust forms on the surface of the wax.

8. Pour in the clear wax, filling the cone.

9. After about 30 minutes, the cooling wax will form a well on the surface. Poke 3 holes in this well with a knitting needle or pencil and refill with hot white wax.

10. Let the wax harden completely, then unmold it. If you have a paper mold, tear it off.

11. Use acrylic paint or highly colored hot wax (see page 78) to paint in the clown's face. Or, if you want, heat the tip of a crayon and use that as a painting tool (see figure 2).

12. Cover the line between the hat and the face sections with a strip of thin wax (see "How to Make Wax Sheets," page 44) or with bright-colored braid glued in place.

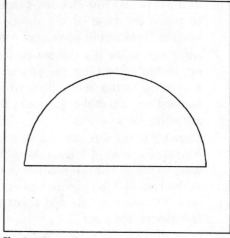

Fig. 1

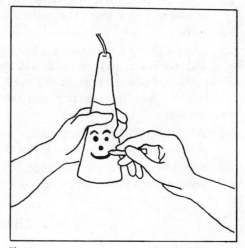

Fig. 2

BIRTHDAY CAKE CANDLE

Ingredients:
Wax: paraffin and stearic acid
Wick: wire-core
Dye: your choice
Scent: your choice
Bowl-shaped mold
Deep container
Eggbeater or fork
Birthday candles and holders
Water bath

1. You will need a round, bowl-shaped mold to make the base of the cake. A small kitchen bowl would work very well.

2. Melt wax, using the double-boiler method, to 180° F. Add the dye of your choice according to the instructions on page 6. Suggestion: a pastel color looks the most attractive for a cake.

3. Pour 1/3 of the wax into a deep container. Add stearic acid (if it is not already in the wax) to the 2/3 of the wax left in the pot, at the rate of 2 tablespoons per pound of wax. At last moment, add scent to both containers (see page 7).

4. Pour the wax containing stearic acid into the lightly greased bowl-shaped mold. After 30 seconds (time to allow the air bubbles to rise) place the mold in a water bath.

5. After about 45 minutes, the cooling wax will contract and form a well on the surface. Poke 3 holes in this well with a knitting needle or pencil and refill with hot wax.

6. When the wax has hardened, invert the mold and release the wax. Insert the wick with a heated skewer (see page 10).

7. Meanwhile, the wax in the deep container should have formed a thin film on the surface. When it does, whip it with an eggbeater or a fork until it is light and frothy.

8. Cover the "cake" with the whipped wax "icing" (see illustration). While it is still warm, insert birthday candle holders.

9. When you light the candle, stick regular birthday candles in the holders and, after they burn down, the center wick will continue burning, probably for the length of the party.

CHRISTMAS TREE CANDLE I

Ingredients:
Wax: paraffin and stearic acid
Wick: wire-core
Dye: green
Scent: pine
Cone-shaped mold
Deep container
Eggbeater or fork
Tree decorations

1. Use a greased pilsner glass or a cone-shaped paper mold to make the tree shape. If you use a paper mold, see instructions on page 60 on how to prepare it and how to insert the wick.

2. Melt wax, using the double-boiler method, to 160° F. Add green dye according to the instructions on page 6.

3. Pour 1/3 of the wax into a deep container. Add stearic acid (if it is not already

in the wax) to the 2/3 of the wax left in the pot, at the rate of 2 tablespoons per pound of wax. Add scent at the last minute to both containers (see page 7).

62

4. If you are using a pilsner glass for a mold, warm it under hot water before pouring the wax (but don't get any water on the inside of the glass). If you are using a paper mold, see step 4 on page 60 for instructions on how to support the mold.

5. Pour the wax containing stearic acid into the cone-shaped mold (see figure 1).

6. After about 30 minutes, the cooling wax will contract and form a well on the surface. Poke 3 holes in this well with a knitting needle or pencil and refill with hot wax.

7. When the wax has hardened, unmold it. If you have used a paper mold, tear it off. if you used a pilsner glass, insert wick now (see page 10).

8. Meanwhile, the wax in the deep container should have formed a thin film on the surface. When it does, whip it with an eggbeater or a fork until it is light and frothy.

9. Press the whipped wax thickly onto the cone-shaped "tree," letting it mound up in places to have a natural look.

10. You can decorate the tree in several ways: sprinkle glitter overall; press sequins into the whipped wax while it is still warm (as pictured in figure 2); press tiny Christmas balls into the warm whipped wax; festoon the tree with tinsel.

Fig. 1

Fig. 2

CHRISTMAS TREE CANDLE II

Ingredients:
Wax: paraffin and stearic acid
Wick: flat- or square-braided
Dye: green
Scent: pine
Cone-shaped mold
Sharp knife
Glue (optional)
Tree decorations

1. Use a greased pilsner glass or a cone-shaped paper cup as a mold. See page 60 on how to prepare a paper mold (but don't insert the wick beforehand).

2. Melt wax, using the double-boiler method, to 160° F. When it is fully melted, add

63

stearic acid (unless it is already in the wax) at the rate of 2 tablespoons per pound of wax. Add green dye according to the instructions on page 6. Finally, add scent (see page 7).

3. If you are using a glass mold, warm it under hot water before pouring the wax into it (but don't get any water on the inside of the glass). See step 4 on page 60 for instructions on how to support a paper mold.

4. Pour the wax into the mold.

5. After about 30 minutes, a well will form on the surface of the cooling wax. Poke 3 holes in this well with a knitting needle or pencil and refill it with hot wax.

6. When the wax has hardened, remove it from the mold. To remove a paper mold, you must tear it off.

7. Make 2 more cones of wax, following steps 3 through 6.

8. Use a sharp knife to cut off the pointed tops of two of the cooled, unmolded cones. You will find, however, that some of the paper cups that can be purchased in supermarkets are already flattened at the bottom, so that if you use these, this step would not be necessary.

9. Heat a skewer and poke a hole down the center of each cone.

10. Tie a knot in 1 end of the wick and

thread the loose end into the hole at the bottom of 1 of the unpointed cones, pulling the wick through to the top. String the next 2 cones in the same way, ending with the pointed cone on top (see illustration).

11. Spread the 2 cut surfaces (the tops of the bottom 2 cones) with white glue or hot (230° F) green wax to hold the 3 cones together. Pull the wick taut.

12. Decorate the tree with spray glitter, tinsel festoons, and/or small circles cut from foil or colored paper (the last two will have to be attached with glue or tiny pins).

SNOWMAN CANDLE

Ingredients:
Wax: paraffin and stearic acid
Wick: flat- or square-braided
Dye: none
Scent: your choice
3 hollow rubber balls
Bowl of water
Single-edged razor blade
Eggbeater or fork
Deep container

64

1. Craft stores sell glass molds for making round candles, but you can make your own out of hollow rubber balls. Ideally, you should have a small, medium, and large ball (for the head, middle, and bottom of the snowman), but 3 balls of the same size can be used instead.

2. Melt wax, using the double-boiler method, to 160°F. Do not add dye.

3. Pour 1/3 of the wax into a separate, deep container. Add stearic acid (if it is not already in the wax) to the 2/3 of the wax left in the pot, at the rate of 2 tablespoons per pound of wax. At the last minute, add scent to both containers (see page 7).

Fig. 1

4. Cut a 3/4-inch-diameter hole in a rubber ball.

5. Float the ball in a container of water, taking care that no water gets inside.

6. Pour the wax carefully into the floating ball (it might help to use a funnel). Steady the ball with your hand as you pour. Take care not to get any hot wax on your hand. The pressure of the water against the rubber ball will work to maintain the ball shape when it is filled with hot wax (see figure 1).

7. After a few minutes, a well will form in the top of the wax. Poke 2 holes in the well with a skewer, then refill with hot wax.

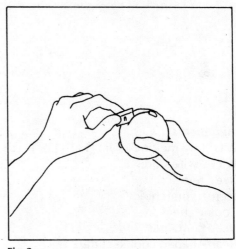

Fig. 2

8. When the wax has cooled, use a single-edged razor blade to cut the rubber away from the wax (see figure 2).

9. Make 2 more balls, following steps 4 through 7.

10. Heat a skewer and poke a hole through the center of each cooled ball.

11. Tie a knot in one end of the wick and thread the loose end into the hole in one of the balls. Pull the wick through the ball and string the next 2 balls onto the wick in the same way. If you have made balls of different sizes, string the large one first, then the medium, and lastly the small.

Fig. 3

12. Spread the surfaces of the balls, where they touch, with white glue or hot (240°F) clear wax to hold the 3 balls together.

13. Meanwhile, the wax in the deep container will have formed a thin skin on the surface. When it does, whip it with an eggbeater or a fork until it is light and frothy.

14. Press the whipped wax "snow" all around the snowman (see figure 3).

15. The features can be bits of colored wax pressed into the "snow," small beads, or paint (see figure 4).

Fig. 4

VALENTINE CANDLE

Ingredients:
Wax: low-melting-point (130°-135°F) paraffin
Wick: wire-core
Dye: red
Scent: your choice
Cookie sheet
Deep container
Heart-shaped cookie cutter
Sharp knife
Round bottle
Eggbeater

1. Melt low-melting-point paraffin (130°-135°F), using the double-boiler method. Do not add stearic acid.

2. Pour 1/4 of the liquid wax into another container and add red dye (see page 6). At last moment, add scent to each container (see page 7).

3. Pour a 1/8-inch-deep wax sheet, using the undyed wax, into the cookie sheet. See page 44, "How to Make Wax Sheets." This will not use up much of the undyed wax, so you will have a lot left in the pot for step 11. Pour this leftover wax into a deep container.

4. Let the wax sheet cool to the point where it cannot be easily dented with a fingertip.

5. Use a heart-shaped cookie cutter to cut out rows of hearts in the wax sheet (while it is still in the cookie sheet). Leave at least 1/4 inch between the hearts (see figure 1).

6. Then pour the red wax (at 160°F) as a second, 1/8-inch layer over the first one.

66

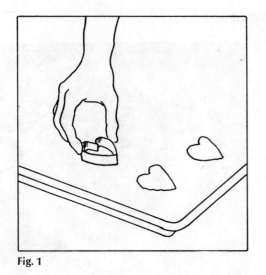
Fig. 1

Fig. 2

The red wax will flow into the cut-out heart shapes as well as leave a thin red layer over the white layer (see figure 2).

7. Let the wax harden, as in step 4.

8. Very carefully cut around the edges of the cookie sheet with a sharp knife and lift out the wax sheet. Make sure not to push through the heart cutouts with your fingertips.

9. Wrap the sheet around the round bottle, red layer against the glass. Trim the edges so that they are even and press them firmly together (see figure 3). If they don't hold well, heat a butter knife and go over the edges with it to seal the seam. Let the wax harden.

Fig. 3

10. Gently lift the bottle out, leaving a cylinder of wax.

11. Meanwhile, the wax left in the deep container will have formed a thin skin on the surface. When it does, whip it with an eggbeater or a fork until it is light and frothy.

12. Fill the cylinder of wax with the whipped wax (see figure 4).

13. While the whipped wax is still warm, insert a wire-core wick (see page 10).

Fig. 4

Ingredients:
Wax: paraffin and stearic acid
Wick: 2 lengths wire-core
Dye: red
Scent: your choice
Heart-shaped candy box or gelatin mold

1. Save a heart-shaped candy box from Valentine's Day for this candle. Or, if you have one, use a heart-shaped gelatin mold. The instructions that follow are for the cardboard type of candy box.

2. Melt wax, using the double-boiler method, at 160°F. When it is fully melted, add stearic acid (if it not already in the wax) at the rate of 2 tablespoons per pound of wax. Add red dye according to the instructions on page 6. Finally, add scent (see page 7).

3. Lightly grease the candy box with cooking oil or silicone mold-release spray.

4. Pour the wax into the candy box (see figure 1). If the box is a shallow one, 1 inch or less in depth, use both the top and the bottom of the box to make 2 layers, which will then be attached together.

5. After about 45 minutes, a small well will form on the surface of the wax. Poke it 3 times with a knitting needle or a pencil and refill it with hot wax.

6. When the wax has hardened, unmold it by tearing off the cardboard.

7. To attach the 2 layers, if you've made 2, brush the surface with hot (240°F) red wax and press them together (see figure 2). Then dip the whole thing in the hot wax, taking care not to burn your fingers.

8. Insert the 2 wicks with a heated skewer (see page 10).

9. A lace border around the candle adds a lovely touch and also covers up any traces of a seam between the 2 layers.

Fig. 1

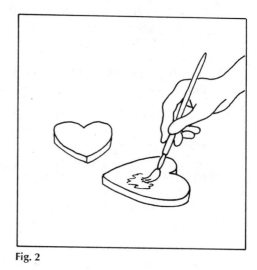

Fig. 2

EASTER EGG CANDLE

Ingredients:
Wax: paraffin and stearic acid
Wick: wire-core
Dye: none
Scent: your choice
Egg
Cardboard egg box
Masking tape

1. Prepare the egg as a mold as follows: Make a 1/2-inch hole in the large end of the egg. Punch a small hole at the other end with a needle. Shake or blow the egg out of the shell. Rinse the shell out with a mixture of warm water and vinegar and let it dry.

2. Carefully enlarge the small hole until it is large enough so that a small-size wire-core wick can fit through.

3. Thread the wick through the shell, leaving about 1/4 inch sticking out at the small end. This is the top of the candle. Place a piece of masking tape over both the hole and the end of the wick to avoid leakage. Push a needle through the other end of the wick and use the needle as a wick support, centered across the top of the shell.

4. Stand the egg, small side down, in the cardboard box in which eggs are sold.

5. Melt wax, using the double-boiler method, and add stearic acid. It takes only about 1/4 to 1/3 cup of wax for each candle. You can possibly use leftover wax for small candles like this. At the last minute, add scent (see page 7).

6. Pour the wax (heated to 160°F) very carefully into the larger hole. You might use an eye dropper or perfume funnel to do this (see figure 1).

7. After a few minutes, a well will form. Poke 2 holes with a slender skewer and refill the well with hot wax. Do this as often as the well forms.

Fig. 1

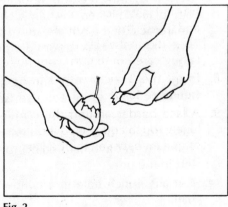

Fig. 2

69

8. When the wax is hard, remove the masking tape and the needle, carefully crack the shell, and then peel it off (see figure 2).

9. Trim the wick at the bottom of the candle (large end). To make a flat bottom for the candle, rotate it gently on a heated pie pan.

10. If the surface of the wax is rough, dip the egg candle quickly into a hot (240°F) wax bath (see page 10).

11. **VARIATION:** Make a white candle, then dip it into a wax bath of a different color.

12. Decorate the egg candle with glued-on sequins (see figure 3) or paint it with wax (see page 78) or with acrylics (see page 82).

Fig. 3

AUTUMN TOMATO CANDLE

Ingredients:
Wax: paraffin and stearic acid
Wick: wire-core
Dye: orange and green
Hollow rubber ball
Bowl of water
Single-edged razor blade
Aluminum foil
Scissors
Wax bath

1. Melt wax, using the double-boiler method, to 160°F. When it is fully melted, add stearic acid (if it is not already in the wax) at the rate of 2 tablespoons per pound of wax.

2. Pour 1/4 cup of wax into a separate container and add green dye (see page 6).

3. Add orange dye (or combine red and yellow to get a tomato color) to the dye left in the pot.

4. Cut a 3/4-inch hole in a hollow rubber ball.

5. Float the ball, hole side up, in a bowl of water. Be very careful to avoid getting any water inside the ball.

6. Gently pour the wax, from a small cup or with an eye dropper, into the ball. Steady the ball with your other hand as you pour. Be careful not to burn yourself with the hot wax.

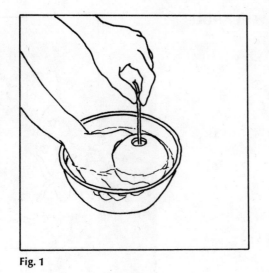

Fig. 1

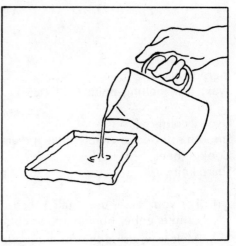

Fig. 2

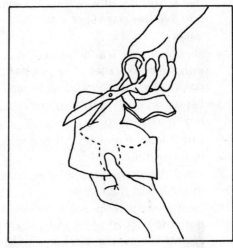

Fig. 3

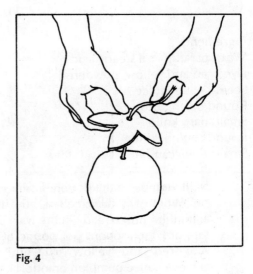

Fig. 4

7. When a crust forms on the surface of the wax, insert a wire-core wick so that at least 3/4 inch of wick is left outside the ball (see figure 1). When a well forms, poke 2 holes with a knitting needle or skewer and refill it with hot wax. Do this as often as the well reappears.

8. While the wax in the ball is cooling, reheat the green-dye wax to 160° F.

9. Fold a small (3-inch-square) sheet of aluminum foil into a tiny pan with an edge all around. Pour the green wax into this aluminum pan so that it is 1/8 to 1/4 inch deep (see figure 2).

10. When the green wax cools, lift it out of the foil and punch a wick hole through the center. Use scissors to cut a leaf shape out of the wax (see figure 3).

11. When the wax in the ball has hardened, cut the rubber away from the wax with a single-edged razor blade.

12. If the wax leaf has stiffened, warm it in steam or warm water. Then place it on the top of the "tomato" by pulling the wick through the center hole. Press the leaf into place against the "tomato" (see figure 4).

13. A quick dip into hot (240° F) clear wax (see page 10), then into room-temperature water, will add gloss as a finishing touch.

AUTUMN LEAVES CANDLE

Ingredients:
Wax: low-melting-point (130°-135°F) paraffin
Dye: 2 colors
Smooth solid-color candle, 3-inch diameter
Cookie sheet
Sharp knife

1. For your base, use a tall 3-inch-diameter candle, either homemade or commercial.
2. Melt wax, using the double-boiler method, to 170°F; do not add stearic acid.
3. To make leaves of more than 1 color, divide the liquid wax into 2 portions and add dye (see page 6) of a different color to each.
4. Slowly pour a 1/8-inch-deep layer of wax into the cookie sheet (see page 44). With 2 colors of wax, use 2 cookie sheets.
5. Let the wax cool until you can't easily dent it with a fingertip.
6. Cut 3 leaf shapes out of the wax sheets (see illustration).
7. Bend the leaves so that they conform to the shape of the candle.
8. Heat clear wax to 240°F. Brush the wax onto the back of a leaf and quickly press it against the candle. Repeat with the other 2 leaves.

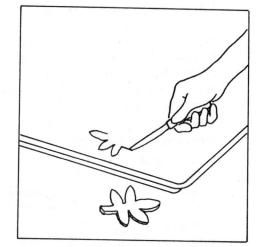

JACK-O'-LANTERN

Ingredients:
Wax: paraffin and stearic acid
Dye: red and yellow, powdered
Scent: your choice
Round mixing bowl
Small sharp knife
Round cookie cutter
Small votive candle

1. Melt wax, using the double-boiler method. When it is fully melted, add stearic acid (if it is not already in the wax) at the rate of 2 tablespoons per pound of wax. Add red and yellow dye until you achieve a nice pumpkin orange.

2. Lightly grease the mixing bowl with oil or silicone mold-release spray.

3. Pour the wax slowly into the bowl.

4. Let the wax stand until a 1/4-inch-thick crust forms on the top and the sides. Use the small knife to cut a circle in the surface, lift it out, and pour off the liquid wax.

5. Let the wax shell cool in the bowl until it is no longer moist. Use the knife to cut 2 triangular holes in the wax, as indicated in figure 1. Then press a round circle with the cookie cutter in the bottom of the bowl.

6. When the wax has fully cooled, unmold it by tapping the bowl, upside down, on a padded surface. Trim the triangular eye holes until they are even.

7. Repeat steps 2, 3, and 4 to form the bottom half of the jack-o'-lantern. This time, instead of eyes, cut a hole or holes for the mouth. Make a round hole in the bottom as in step 5 (see figure 2). Then unmold.

8. Trim the edges of each half so they are even and fit together smoothly.

9. Heat the small knife and run it over the edges to secure the two halves together. You will have to do this very carefully, reheating the knife several times (see figure 3).

10. If you have any orange wax left over, heat it slightly and roll the seam of your pumpkin in it to seal the seam even more.

11. Sprinkle red and brown powdered dye, from shakers (see page 50) around the top of the jack-o'-lantern. Then lightly go over the surface with a butane torch.

12. A final spray with silicone will make the jack-o'-lantern seem even more glossy.

13. Use a votive candle placed in the hole at center bottom to illuminate the jack-o'-lantern. The hole at the top will release the heat.

Fig. 1

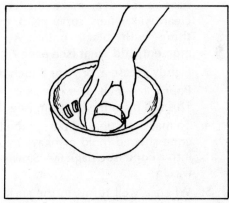

Fig. 2

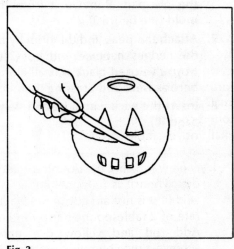

Fig. 3

Ingredients:
Wax: paraffin and stearic acid
Wick: wire-core
Dye: black (optional)
Scent: your choice
7- or 8-inch pie pan
Cone-shaped mold
Black spray paint (optional)

1. Melt wax, using the double-boiler method. When it is fully melted, add stearic acid (if it is not already in the wax) at the rate of 2 tablespoons per pound of wax. Add black dye (see page 6). If you don't have black dye, make the candle with clear wax, then spray-paint the whole thing with black paint. At the last moment, add scent (see page 7).

2. Lightly grease a or 7- or 8-inch pie pan

3. Pour a 1/4-inch layer of wax into the pan. This will form the hat brim (see figure 1).

4. To make the peaked part of the hat, use a cone-shaped mold or heavy paper rolled into a cone (see page 60). Slowly pour the wax in.

5. When a well forms in the surface of the wax in the cone, after about 45 minutes, poke 3 holes in it with a knitting needle or pencil and refill with hot wax.

6. When the wax has hardened, tap it out of the pie pan. Remove it from the cone mold (see figure 2).

7. Attach the peak and the brim by brushing the 2 edges that meet with hot (240°F) wax (if you've used black wax all along, use it here as well) and pressing them together.

8. Insert the wick with a heated skewer (see page 10).

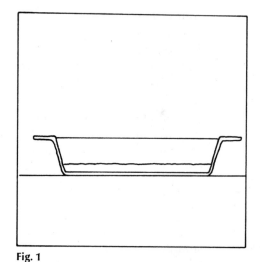

Fig. 1

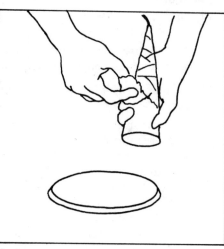

Fig. 2

GARDEN FLARE

Ingredients:
Wax: leftover paraffin
Wick: carton twine or rope
Dye: black
Scent: citronella
Ceramic plant pot
Masking tape

1. Making this candle is best when you've accumulated lots of scrap wax, leftovers from previous candlemaking or leavings of candles already melted.

2. Melt all the scraps together, using the double-boiler method. The mixture of colors should turn the wax a dark brown or black. If not, add black dye according to the instructions on page 6. Do not add stearic acid.

3. Add citronella scent, a known mosquito repellent.

4. This will be a container candle, which means that it will not be unmolded. Use an ordinary ceramic plant pot for a container.

5. Heavy carton twine or rope should be used as a wick. Thread the wick through the hole in the bottom of the pot and secure it in place with masking tape on the outside (see figure 1). Set the pot on a piece of heavy cardboard.

6. Tie the loose end of the wick around a pencil and center the pencil across the top of the pot.

7. Pour a small pool of wax into the bottom of the pot, to harden and hold the wick in place (see figure 2).

8. Then slowly pour the rest of the wax into the pot.

9. After about 45 minutes, a well will form on the surface of the wax. Poke 3 holes in this well with a knitting needle or pencil and refill with hot wax. Do this as often as the well forms.

10. The candle, when hardened, can be placed outdoors on a patio or lawn. It is perfect for parties, since it keeps the bugs away while providing a romantic glow.

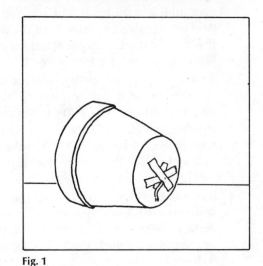

Fig. 1

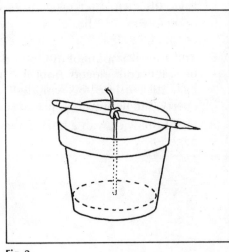

Fig. 2

ICE-CREAM-SODA CANDLE*

Ingredients:
Wax: paraffin and stearic acid
Wick: wire-core
Dye: orange and red
Scent: your choice
Ice-cream-soda glass
Deep container
Eggbeater or fork

* Calvin Sternberg, Cornwells Hgts., Pennsylvania

1. Melt wax, using the double-boiler method. When it is fully melted, pour 1/4 of the wax into a deep container. Add stearic acid (if it is not already in the wax) to the wax left in the pot at the rate of 2 tablespoons per pound of wax. Pour 1/4 cup of wax into a small bowl and add red dye. Add orange dye (see page 6) to the wax in the pot. At the last moment, add scent to all containers of dye (see page 7).

2. Warm the outside of the soda glass by running it under warm water, but be careful not to get any water in the glass.

3. Holding the glass at a tilt, slowly pour the orange wax, heated to 170°F, to a level 1/2 inch from the top of the glass (see figure 1).

4. Meanwhile, the wax left in the deep container will have formed a skin on the surface. When it does, beat it with an eggbeater or a fork until it is light and fluffy.

5. Layer the whipped wax on top of the orange wax in the glass as "whipped cream."

6. Roll a small amount of the cooled red wax between your fingers until it is a round ball. Stick it into the whipped wax as a cherry (see figure 2).

7. Insert the wick with a heated skewer (see page 10).

Fig. 1

Fig. 2

FOURTH-OF-JULY STROBE

Ingredients:
Wax: paraffin and stearic acid
Wick: dental cotton
Dye: red and blue
Scent: your choice
Paper cup
Wire

1. Melt wax, using the double-boiler method, to 160° F. When it is fully melted, add stearic acid (if it is not already in the wax) at the rate of 2 tablespoons per pound of wax. Do not add dye, but pour 1/3 of the wax into a different pot. Add scent to containers of wax at last moment (see page 7).

2. Reinforce the sides of a paper cup with masking tape to brace it as a mold.

3. Ask your dentist for a short roll of cotton, or get it at a drugstore, to be used as the wick, creating a strobe effect. Insert a thin piece of wire down the length of the wick to hold it straight (see figure 1).

4. Stand the wick in the paper cup. If it doesn't remain upright, brace it with a pencil laid across the top of the cup.

5. Pour the wax (the 2/3 left in the pot) into the mold.

6. After about 45 minutes a well will form around the wick on the surface of the wax. Poke 3 holes in the well with a knitting needle or pencil and refill with hot clear wax.

7. When the wax has fully hardened, tear away the cup.

8. Divide the 1/3 of the wax that you have left into two portions. Add red dye to one portion and blue dye to the other (see page 6).

9. Hold the candle by the wick and dip the other end into the red wax so that 1/3 of the candle is covered. Dip in and out quickly until you get a clear red band of color. Remove the wire from the wick.

10. When the red wax has dried, hold the candle by that end and dip the other end into the blue wax. Again, dip only 1/3 of the candle. Dip until you get a clear blue band of color. See Figure 2.

Fig. 1

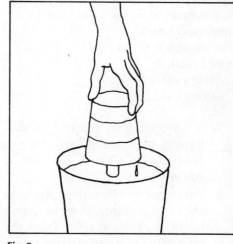

Fig. 2

CHAPTER SEVEN

PAINTED AND DECOUPAGE CANDLES

WAX-PAINTED CANDLES

Ingredients:

Wax: paraffin

Dye: as many colors as you need for your design

Smooth solid-colored candle

Masking tape

Shallow pan to hold hot water

Tiny containers to hold wax "paint"

Small paintbrush

Tracing paper

Lead pencil

Knitting needle

Cleaning fluid

1. A smooth solid-colored candle, store-bought or homemade, is necessary as a base candle. Choose any size of candle you want.

2. It is sometimes helpful to plan your design ahead of painting time, unless you are a talented freehand artist. Draw the design on a piece of tracing paper, then turn the paper over and go over the lines with a soft lead pencil. Next, with masking tape, tape the paper to the candle, lead side against the wax, and trace the lines with a knitting needle. The lead will be pressed onto the candle, providing you with an outline. A simpler method would be to

78

sketch your design lightly on the candle, but remember that erasing is impossible.

3. Melt wax, using the double-boiler method. Do not add stearic acid.

4. When the wax is fully melted, pour it into as many small containers (such as egg poachers, tiny pastry tins, bottle caps) as you want colors. The wax for painting must be highly concentrated in color, so use a ratio of 1 part dye to 4 parts clear wax. Add the dye to the small containers of wax.

5. Place the small containers of wax in a shallow pan of hot water. (Be careful not to allow the water to get in the wax.) Keep the water hot by putting the pan over a low heat, or else your wax will become too hard to paint with (see figure 1).

6. Use a small brush to paint the wax onto the candle. You will find that the deeper you dip into your wax-melting containers, the darker the color of the wax (see figure 2).

7. To remove wax from your brushes, dip them in boiling water for a few moments, wipe them with tissue, then dip in cleaning fluid.

Fig. 1

Fig. 2

WAX-DRIPPED CANDLE*

* W. Spencer, Inc., Portland, Maine

Ingredients:
Wax: paraffin
Dye: as many colors as you want
Smooth candle
Spoon
Wax bath

1. The base candle for this method of decorating may be store-bought or your own. If you make it yourself, use an extra-long wick (at least 3 inches showing outside the candle) so that you will easily be able to dip the candle in hot wax.

2. If you have wax left over from previous candlemaking sessions, use it to make the drips. If you must start from scratch, melt the wax as usual, using the double-boiler method. Do not add stearic acid. Divide

the wax into as many containers as you want colors, then add a different color dye to each.

3. Spoon different colors of liquid wax (at 170°F) over the candle and let them drip down the sides, as in the ball candle in the photograph (see figure 1).

4. A second method of dripping is to hold the candle on its side, spoon the liquid wax onto it, and then rotate it. The second method gives you horizontal drips, as in the cube candle (see figure 2).

5. Let the candle and drips set for about 1/2 minute, then dip the candle into clear wax (with a melting point of 133°F) heated to 180°-190°F. This step is essential in order to keep the wax dribbles from chipping off. Immediately after the hot wax, dip the candle in room-temperature water, which will add gloss.

6. An alternative method of setting the dripped wax to that described in step 5 is to dip the candle into a very hot (240°F) clear wax bath (see page 10). The hotter wax will cause the dribbled wax to melt and run together in an artistic way, as in the pillar candle in the photograph. The same effect can be achieved by running the flame of a butane torch quickly over the candle. Continue with a room-temperature water dip, as before.

Fig. 1

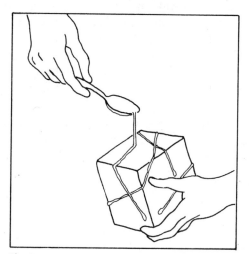

Fig. 2

SPONGE-PAINTED CANDLE

Ingredients:
Wax: paraffin
Dye: 2 colors
Smooth candle
2 muffin tins
2 sponges
Butane torch

1. A smooth solid-colored candle, store-bought or homemade, is necessary as a base candle.

2. Melt wax, using the double-boiler method. Do not add stearic acid.

3. Pour the wax into 2 small containers, such as muffin tins or coffee cups.

4. Select 2 colors that blend well together and add 1 color dye to each container. The wax must be highly concentrated in color, so add dye with a ratio of 1 part dye to 4 parts wax.

5. Keep the wax warm by placing the containers in a shallow pan of water over low heat. Be careful not to get water in the containers.

6. Dip a corner of 1 of the sponges into a container and then press it against the base candle (see illustration). Continue this 'process, pressing in random spots, until the candle has a somewhat patchy but good coating of wax.

7. Dip the second sponge into the other color of wax and repeat step 6.

8. Let the wax dry, then torch it lightly with a butane torch so that the colored wax is fixed to the candle.

SWIRL-PAINTED CANDLE

Ingredients:
Smooth solid-colored candle
Oil paints
Deep bucket of water
Spoon

1. Select 2 or 3 different colors of oil paints that complement each other.

2. Fill a deep bucket with room-temperature water.

3. Carefully spoon drops of the different colored paints onto the surface of the water. You must do this gently, sliding the paint off the spoon, or the drops might sink to the bottom (see figure 1).

4. Stir the water, again gently, so that it begins a slight swirl.

5. Hold the smooth solid-colored candle by its wick and dip it into the center of the swirling paint, then lift it out (see figure 2).

6. Let the paint dry thoroughly, perhaps even overnight, before attempting to handle the candle.

Fig. 1

Fig. 2

ACRYLIC-PAINTED CANDLE

Ingredients:
Smooth solid-colored candle
Acrylic paint
Masking tape

1. Acrylic paints, thinned with a little water, work quite well in decorating candles. You can use the method for transferring, described on page 78, for both acrylic- and wax-painted candles. The candle on this page does not need artistic ability.
2. Use a smooth solid-colored candle as a base candle.
3. Cut 2 lengths of masking tape and criss-cross them over the top of the candle, as illustrated in figure 1.
4. Paint the uncovered portions of the wax with acrylic paint (see figure 2).
5. When the paint dries, remove the tape.

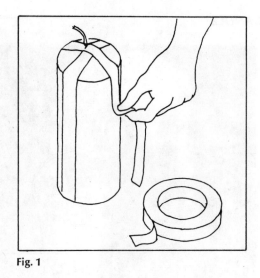

Fig. 1

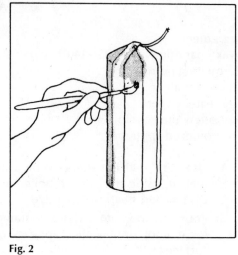

Fig. 2

DOILY CANDLE

Ingredients:
Smooth solid-colored candle
Large lace doily
Tape
Can of spray paint

1. Wrap a large lace doily around a round candle, taping the edges to the candle.

2. Spray paint, whatever color you desire, and from a fairly good distance, over the candle. The cut-out designs on the doily will be the painted areas on the candle (see illustration).

3. To get good coverage, 2 or 3 coats of paint are necessary.

4. When the paint has dried thoroughly, remove the doily, leaving a delicately painted candle.

83

APPLIQUÉ CANDLE

Ingredients:
Wax: paraffin with a 133°-140° F
    melting point
Deep container
Eggbeater or fork
Smooth white candle
Embroidered appliqué

1. Use 133°-140°F-melting-point wax and melt it, using the double-boiler method. Do not add stearic acid or dye.

2. Pour the wax into a deep container and let it cool until a film appears on the surface.

3. Use an eggbeater or a fork to whip the wax until it becomes fluffy.

4. Cover the smooth white core candle with the whipped wax, taking care to keep the wick uncovered (see figure 1).

5. While the wax is still soft, press an embroidered appliqué against it. Hold the appliqué in place with your fingers until the wax hardens enough to support it (see figure 2).

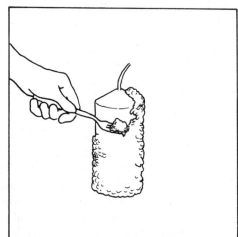

Fig. 1

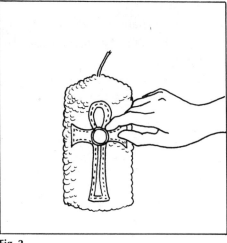

Fig. 2

84

DECOUPAGE CANDLE

Ingredients:
Smooth candle
A piece for decoupage
Iron (optional)
Wax bath

A charming illustration from a greeting card, an attractive print, an interesting wrapping-paper design—any of these can be used to adorn a candle. On this page are two methods of doing so.

A.

1. Select a candle large enough to hold the picture you have chosen. This can be either a candle of your own making or a store-bought one.

2. Cut out the picture you are going to use, trimming off unnecessary edges. Singed edges frequently look quite attractive.

3. Brush hot (240°F) wax on the back of the picture (see figure 1) and press it quickly against the candle.

4. Dip the candle into a hot (240°F) clear wax bath (see page 10) to coat the picture with wax. If the candle is tall, dip first one end, then turn it over and dip the other end.

B.

1. and 2. The steps are the same as in previous method.

3. Set an ordinary iron on medium heat. Hold the picture against the candle and iron over it until the candle wax flows over the picture, sealing it in place (see figure 2).

4. To remove the wax from the iron, pass iron over absorbent paper towels.

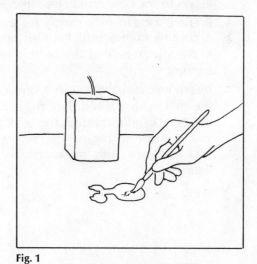

Fig. 1

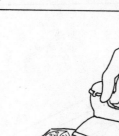

Fig. 2

85

PLASTIC-FLOWER CANDLE

Ingredients:
Wax: paraffin
Dye: your choice
2-inch-diameter-core candle
Plastic flowers
Small pins
Milk carton
Masking tape
Water bath

1. Make or buy a 2-inch-diameter tubular candle to use as a core.
2. Select an attractive plastic flower or leaf (or several) that you think would look well in a candle. Relatively flat flowers work best.
3. Use small pins to attach the flowers and leaves to the core candle (see figure 1).
4. Prepare a quart milk carton for a mold according to the instructions on page 15. Make a wick hole in the bottom of the carton.
5. Insert the core candle, upside down, into the milk carton mold. Pull the wick of the core candle through the wick hole you've made in the carton. Secure the wick in place with masking tape (see figure 2).

Fig. 1

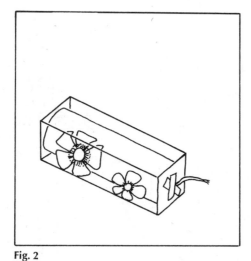

Fig. 2

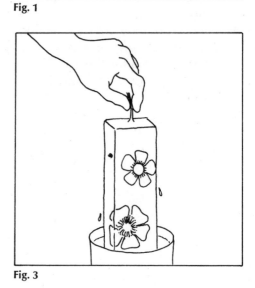

Fig. 3

6. Melt wax, using the double-boiler method. Do not add stearic acid, since the wax should be translucent for the best effect. Add the dye of your choice (see page 6).

7. Pour the wax, at 170°F, into the area between the core candle and the mold wall.

8. Place the mold in a room-temperature water bath.

9. When the wax has cooled, tear off the carton.

10. The bottom of your candle may be uneven; if so, rotate it on a heated pie pan.

11. If you want the flowers to protrude, place the candle in hot water for a few seconds, or as long as needed (see figure 3).

CHAPTER EIGHT

MODERN CANDLES

LAYERED CANDLE

Ingredients:
Wax: paraffin and stearic acid
Wick: flat- or square-braided
Dye: at least 2 colors
Scent: your choice
Mold: milk carton used in examples

1. Select a mold. If you use a milk carton for a mold, reinforce it by taping it with masking tape at the top, middle and bottom. See page 15 for detailed instructions on reinforcing the carton.

2. Insert the wick: punch a small hole through the bottom of the carton and string the wick through it. Tie a knot at the bottom of the wick outside the hole and cover the hole and the knot with masking tape, to prevent wax leakage. Tie the top end of the wick to a pencil and center the pencil across the top of the carton.

3. Melt the wax, using the double-boiler

method; when it is fully melted, add stearic acid at the rate of 2 tablespoons per pound of wax (that is, if it is not already in the wax).

4. To make a 2-color layered candle, divide the liquid wax into 2 containers and add

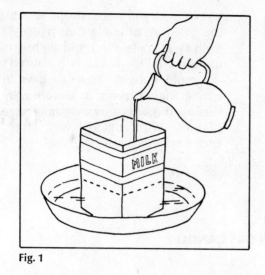

Fig. 1

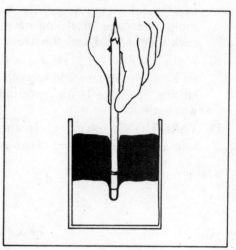

Fig. 2

a different color dye to each container. See page 6 for instructions on the use of dye. Add scent at the last moment (see page 7).

5. When you are using a milk-carton mold, the wax should not be hotter than 160°F when you pour. When you have a metal mold, pour the wax at 200°F. Hold the mold upright and pour the first color of wax *slowly* into the center. Don't let the wax run down the side of the mold because it might stick to the side in places, causing the second layer to have streaks of the first layer's color (see figure 1).

6. Let the first layer air-cool until a crust forms on the top. If you let each layer get too cold, the wax will shrink and there will be a ridge between the colors.

7. When the crust has formed, pour in your second layer of color at 200°F (160°F in milk cartons). Poke a hole down through the 2 layers, using a pencil (see figure 2).

8. Repeat steps 5, 6, and 7 until your candle is the height you desire. A slight well will form on the surface of the top layer as the wax cools. Poke 3 holes in the well with a pencil or knitting needle and refill it with hot wax of the last color poured (see figure 3).

9. When the wax has hardened, release it from the mold by untying the knot in the wick and inverting the mold. If you have

Fig. 3

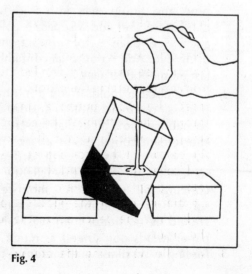

Fig. 4

89

trouble releasing the candle from the mold, see page 10. If you have used a milk-carton mold, tear the paper off.

10. A dip in a hot (240°F) clear wax bath will add a glossy surface and smooth irregularities. See page 10 for more details on wax baths.

11. **VARIATIONS:** You can get an interesting effect by tilting the mold as you pour the layers. You will need props to support the mold at an angle (see figure 4). At each layer, raise the mold slightly more upright until the last layer is poured with the mold upright. You can have alternating angled layers, as pictured, by reversing the angle of the mold at each pouring. With angled layers, insert the wick after the candle is unmolded.

CONCENTRIC-COLORS CANDLE

Ingredients:
Wax: paraffin and stearic acid
Wick: wire-core
Dye: at least 3 colors
Scent: your choice
Round mold
Small knife

1. Melt the wax, using the double-boiler method. When it is fully melted, add stearic acid at the rate of 2 tablespoons per pound of wax (if it is not already in the wax).

2. You will need several colors of wax for this candle (the one illustrated was made with 5 different colored waxes). If you have leftover wax from previous candlemaking, this might be a good time to use it. If you are starting from scratch, pour the liquid wax into 5 different containers, and add a separate color to each. See page 6 for instructions on using dye. Add scent to all containers at last moment (see page 7).

3. Pick a circular mold. If you don't have a professional metal mold, consider using an oatmeal box, a circular ice-cream or sour-cream container, or a large paper cup. With any of these cardboard molds, remember to grease them lightly with cooking oil or silicone mold-release spray before pouring the wax (which should be no hotter than 160°F). Heavy paper molds don't need as much reinforcing as do flimsy milk cartons.

Fig. 1

90

4. Slowly pour the first color of wax into the mold, filling it.

5. Let the wax cool just enough to form a 1/4-inch crust against the sides of the mold and across the top. The center should still be fluid.

6. Take a small knife and cut a circle through the crust at the top, leaving a 1/4-inch rim (see figure 1). Lift the wax circle out of the way and pour out the fluid wax, leaving a thin wax shell (see figure 2).

7. Allow the shell to cool.

8. Pour a second color of wax into the shell, maintaining the stream of wax down the center. Any hot wax hitting the side of the shell will melt it in patches (see figure 3).

9. Repeat steps 5, 6, and 7 for successive color shells.

10. When the opening left on the surface of the mold is about 1 inch across, insert a wire-core wick.

11. Pour the last color, filling the opening.

12. When the wax is completely cool, release it from the mold. If you have used a cardboard container, tear off the cardboard.

13. If you have been a bit sloppy in pouring the separate colors, it might be necessary to trim the top of the candle with a small knife in order to get clear color definition (see figure 4).

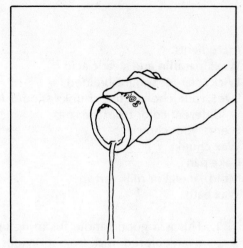

Fig. 2

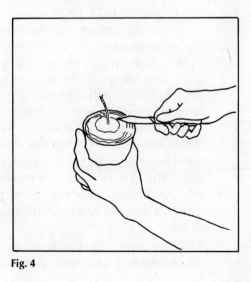

Fig. 3

Fig. 4

91

CHUNK CANDLE*

Ingredients:
Wax: paraffin and stearic acid
Wick: flat- or square-braided
Dye: your choice (the chunks should be a
  different color from the rest)
Scent: your choice
Wax chunks
Cake pan
Mold: metal or milk carton
Wax bath

* Corona International, Hackensack, New Jersey

1. This is a good candle for using up left-over colored wax from previous creations. Just break up the remnants and use them for chunks.

2. To make chunks especially for this candle, use the following procedure:

    A. Melt the wax, using the double-boiler method. When the wax is fully melted, add stearic acid (if it is not already in the wax) at the rate of 2 tablespoons per pound of wax. Add dye according to the instructions on page 6. Lastly, add scent (see page 7).

    B. Pour the wax into a cake pan to a depth of 1/2 inch.

    C. When the wax is firm, yet still warm, cut it into small chunks with a butter knife (see figure 1).

    D. Drop the chunks into a pot of room-temperature water so that they harden and don't stick together. The chunks should be thoroughly dry, however, before coming in contact with hot wax.

3. With a metal mold, secure the wick in place according to the instructions on page 8. With a milk carton, tie the wick around one of the chunks and drop that end into the mold. Tie the other end to a pencil and center it across the top of the mold (see figure 2). Reinforce the carton according to the instructions on page 15.

4. Pile the chunks into the mold, taking care that the wick remains straight up the center.

5. Melt wax, using the double-boiler method. When it is fully melted, add stearic

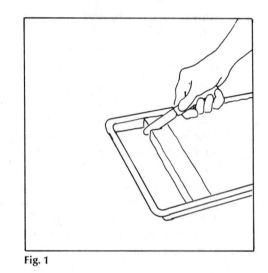

Fig. 1

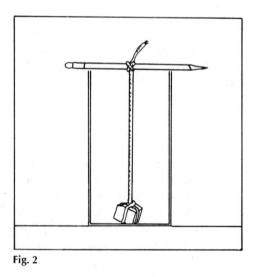

Fig. 2

acid at the rate of 2 tablespoons per pound of wax (if it is not already in the wax). Pick a color that will look well with the chunks you've made and add the appropriate dye (see page 6). If you wish, add scent at the last moment (see page 7).

6. Pour the wax, heated to 200°F (160°F for milk cartons), into the mold (see figure 3). You will see that the smaller chunks tend to melt and distribute their color more than do the larger ones.

7. Have some extra chunks handy, since the chunks settle as the hot wax is poured over them.

8. Place the mold in a water bath of room-temperature water to cool.

9. A small well may form after about 45 minutes. Poke 2 or 3 holes in this well with a knitting needle or a pencil and refill well with hot wax.

10. When the wax has completely hardened, unmold the candle. If you have used a milk carton, tear off the paper.

11. You might find that the colors of the chunks don't show up well because they are covered with a thin layer of wax from the bulk of the candle. Remedy this by dipping the candle into a pot of hot

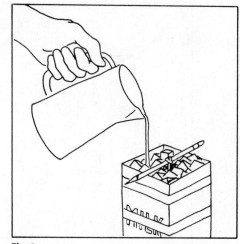

Fig. 3

(240°F) clear wax (see page 10). The hot wax will dissolve the thin layer that mars the appearance of your candle.

12. **VARIATION:** If you want to have a candle with chunks that protrude, make the chunks with wax of a higher melting point than the wax you use for the filler. For example, use 160°F-melting-point wax for the chunks, 130°F-melting-point wax for the filler. Then dip the candle, when hard, in and out of a hot water bath (180°F) to make the filler melt and the chunks protrude more.

LAYERED CHUNK CANDLE

Ingredients:
Wax: paraffin and stearic acid
Wick: wire-core
Dye: 3 colors
Scent: your choice
Wax chunks
Cake pan
1/2-gallon milk carton
Wax bath

1. Melt wax for the chunks, using the double-boiler method. When it is fully melted, add stearic acid at the rate of 2 tablespoons per pound of wax (unless it is already in the wax). Add dye according to the instructions on page 6. Lastly, just before pouring, add scent (see page 7).

2. Pour wax to a depth of 1/2 inch into a

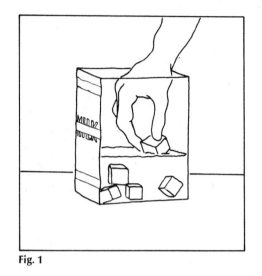

Fig. 1

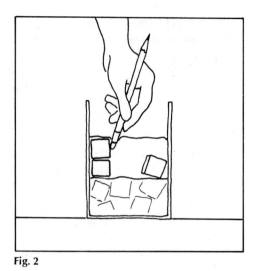

Fig. 2

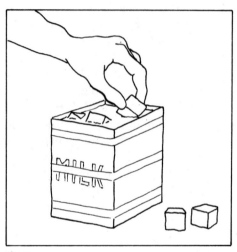

Fig. 3

cake pan. After the wax cools somewhat, cut it into 2-inch chunks with a butter knife. Put the chunks into a pot of room-temperature water to harden.

3. Melt wax for the body of the candle, using the double-boiler method. When it is fully melted, add stearic acid at the rate of 2 tablespoons per pound of wax (unless it is already in the wax).

4. Prepare a 1/2-gallon milk carton for a mold according to the instructions on **page 15**. Place the carton in a pan with 2 inches of cool water at the bottom, in case the seams leak.

5. Pour 1/3 of the wax into a separate container and add the first color dye (see **page 6**). Pour this wax, heated to 180°F, into the carton, filling 1/3 of the mold.

6. Add 1/3 of the chunks to the carton and push them with a stick or pencil so that they touch the sides of the mold. After the wax cools somewhat, add a few more chunks around the edge so that they are only half submerged in the wax (see figure 1).

7. Reheat the rest of the wax to 180°F and add dye of the second color. When the wax in the mold has formed a crust, pour 1/2 of the second-color wax into a separate container. Pour this wax on top of the first layer. Add 1/2 of the chunks that remain.

8. Again, push the chunks so that they rest against the side of the mold (see figure

Fig. 4

2). When the wax has cooled a bit, add a few more chunks around the edges.

9. Continue steps 7 and 8 for the third layer. Add extra chunks so that they stick out on top (see figure 3).

10. After the wax has completely cooled, tear the carton off.

11. You can level the bottom of the candle by rotating it on a heated pie pan.

12. Using a heated barbecue skewer, poke a hole in the candle for the wick. If you want the candle to last for a long time, make it a short wick. After the wick has burned a shallow hole in the candle and is used up, replace it with a small votive candle.

13. You might find that the wax has seeped between the chunks and the mold wall so that the colored chunks don't show up. Remedy this by dipping the candle slowly in hot (240°F) clear wax until enough of the wax on the outside melts away to reveal the chunks (see figure 4). (See page 10 for more details on wax baths.)

ICE-CUBE CANDLE*

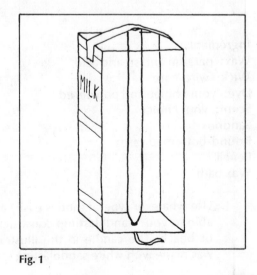

* Corona International, Hackensack, New Jersey

Ingredients:
Wax: paraffin and stearic acid
Dye: your choice
Scent: your choice
Bucket of ice cubes
Slender taper for core candle
Metal mold or quart milk carton

1. Get a bucket of ice cubes. The smaller the pieces of ice, the lacier the effect of your candle.

2. Use a regular taper or dinner candle, upside down, as the wick. Scrape the top of the taper so that you have at least 1 inch of wick to work with. If you are using a metal mold, tie the wick at the top of the candle through the wick hole at the bottom of the mold. Center the other end of the candle with masking tape in the open end of the mold (see figure 1).

3. If you are using a milk-carton mold, punch a hole through the bottom of the carton, thread the wick (of the taper) through it, and tie a knot. Center the candle in the carton by taping it in place at the bottom. Reinforce the carton with masking tape at the top, middle, and bottom—this will prevent leakage and bulging at the seams.

4. Heat the wax, using the double-boiler method, to 230°F. If you are using a milk carton, heat the wax to only 180°F. Add

MILK

Fig. 1

95

stearic acid, if it is not already in the wax, at the rate of 2 tablespoons per pound of wax. Add dye (see page 6 for instructions). At the last moment, add scent (see page 7).

5. Pack the ice cubes tightly around the taper in the mold, making sure that the taper remains centered (see figure 2).

6. Pour out any accumulated water.

7. Pour the melted wax into the mold (see figure 3).

8. You do not need a water bath for this candle, nor will you need to refill the well.

9. When the candle has hardened, pour off the melted water and unmold the candle. If you have used a milk carton, tear it off.

10. **VARIATION:** An interesting effect can be gained by filling the holes left by the ice cubes with hot wax of a different color.

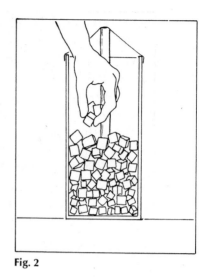

Fig. 2

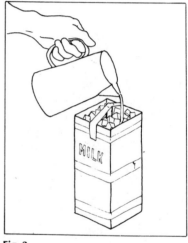

Fig. 3

SAND CANDLE*

Ingredients:
Wax: paraffin and stearic acid
Wick: wire-core
Dye: your choice and powdered
Scent: your choice
Sandbox
Round-bottomed vase
Pencil
Wax bath

1. Use whatever type of sand is easily available to you—sandblasting, construction, or beach. The candle in the illustration was made with white sandblasting sand.

* W. Spencer, Inc., Portland, Maine

96

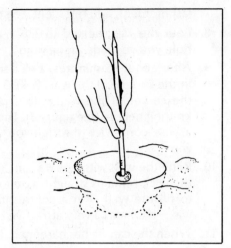
Fig. 1

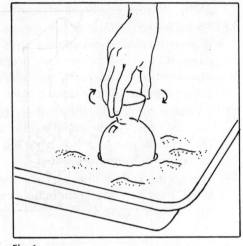

Fig. 2

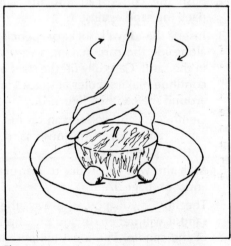
Fig. 3

Fig. 4

2. Dampen the sand and mound it up in a large carton or a dishpan.

3. Use a round-bottomed vase or pitcher (a round chemistry beaker was used for the illustration) to push a round indentation in the sand. Press it firmly and twirl it to make a firm bowl shape (see figure 1). Then lift the vase out.

4. Use a pencil or a long projection bulb to poke 3 legs in the base of the bowl shape. When you use a pencil, twirl it around to make the holes larger than a pencil in width (see figure 2).

5. In order to make the candle illustrated, you will need wax heated to a very hot 230°F. Since a double boiler limits you to a heat of 212°F, the wax for this candle must be melted in a pot directly over the heat. Be extremely careful when melting the wax to avoid scorching or burning. When the wax is fully melted, add stearic acid at the rate of 2 tablespoons per pound of wax (if it is not already in the wax).

6. If the sand in your sandbox is dark in color, this is a good opportunity for you to use up scraps of leftover wax. Melt them to use for the first layer of wax, then finish the pouring with a second layer of dyed wax. The dark sand will hide the first layer from view.

7. For one color of wax throughout, add the dye to the melted wax according to the instructions on page 6. At the very

last moment, add the scent (see page 7).

8. Pour the wax, heated to 230°F, into the hole you've made in the sand.

9. After about 45 minutes, a well will form in the surface of the wax. Poke 3 holes in the center of the well with a pencil or knitting needle (see figure 3). Then insert a wire-core wick through the crust of wax.

10. Refill the well with hot wax, making sure the wick remains straight. You may want to fill the well with a contrasting color wax—it creates a very attractive effect.

11. When the candle has hardened, lift it out of the sandbox and brush off loose sand.

12. Sprinkle the surface of the candle with different colored powdered dyes (see **page 50** for instructions on preparing powdered dye shakers). Then glaze the colors together with a butane torch.

13. To make the sand tightly adhere to the wax, dip the candle quickly into a hot (240°F) clear wax bath (see page 10), then into room-temperature water.

14. The candle will tilt if its legs are uneven. Level them by rotating them on a heated pie pan (see figure 4).

SAND CANDLE VARIATIONS

(A) Coffee Can Sand Candle

Ingredients:
Wax: paraffin and stearic acid
Wick: wire-core
Dye: your choice
Scent: your choice
Sandbox
Coffee can
Dowel stick or thick pencil

1. Make a mound of damp sand in a large carton or dishpan.

2. Push the coffee can into the sand and pack the sand against it.

3. Insert the dowel stick or pencil down alongside the can, making a vertical hole in the sand. Carefully lift the stick out and continue making holes at spaced intervals around the can (see figure 1).

4. Gently ease the coffee can up out of the sand. Tamp down the loose sand at the bottom (see figure 2).

5. Melt the wax according to instructions 5 and 7 on page 97.

6. The hotter you pour the wax, the more sand it will penetrate and pick up as part of the candle. The ideal temperature for this candle (center) is 220°F. The candle

Fig. 1

on the left was poured at 200°F; consequently almost no sand adhered to the wax. The candle on the right was poured at 240°F and picked up more sand than was wanted.

7. Pour the wax into the hole and continue with instructions 9, 10, 11, and 13 on page 98.

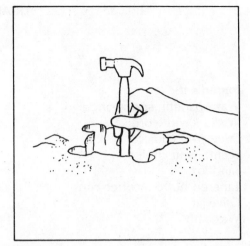

Fig. 2

(B) Octopus Candle

Ingredients:
Wax: paraffin and stearic acid
Wick: wire-core
Dye: your choice
Scent: your choice
Sandbox
Coffee can or small jar
Pencil

1. Make a mound of damp sand in a large carton or dishpan.

2. Press a coffee can or a small jar into the sand to make an indentation; then lift it out.

3. Use a pencil to poke deep thin holes around the sides of the indentation (see illustration).

4. Melt the wax according to instructions 5 and 7 on page 97.

5. Pour the wax at 220°F. You will find that the wax cools as it reaches the ends of the holes, so that less sand will adhere to the protruding parts.

6. Continue with instructions 9, 10, 11, and 13 on page 98.

7. When the candle is taken out of the sand, you will end up with a circular candle having tentacles sticking out from it.

8. **VARIATION:** Break off the tentacles and smooth off the rough edges. You will end up with a sand candle having large wax polka dots.

TRIANGLE SAND CANDLE*

Ingredients:
Wax: paraffin and stearic acid
Wick: 2 wire-core
Dye: your choice
Scent: your choice
Sandbox
Tapered-bottom coffee cups
Olive jar
Wax bath

1. Use whatever type of sand is easily available to you—sandblasting, construction, or beach. The candle in the illustration was made with white sandblasting sand, which gives a lovely effect when the candle is lit.

2. Dampen the sand and pack it firmly into a large carton or dishpan.

3. Use coffee cups that taper to a base (not mugs) to press 3 holes in the sand. Arrange the holes so that they will be the points of your triangle, about 4 inches apart from each other (see figure 1).

4. You will need a narrow bottle at least 4 inches in height for the next step. A thin jar such as one that olives come in would work well. Press this jar into the sand to make connecting troughs between the 3 holes (see figure 2).

5. Use the bowl of a spoon or your fingers to pack the edges of the troughs smooth (see figure 3).

6. In order to make the candle as illustrated, you will need wax heated to a very hot 240°F. Since a double boiler limits you to a heat of 212°F, the wax for this candle must be melted in a pot directly over the heat. Do this *very* carefully so that you avoid scorching or burning the wax. If, however, you would like a candle with only a little sand sticking to it, you can pour the wax at 200°F and so can use the double-boiler method after all.

7. When the wax is fully melted, add stearic acid at the rate of 2 tablespoons per

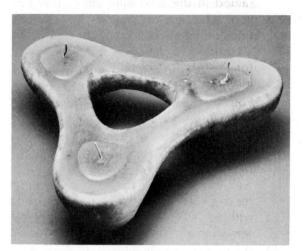

* W. Spencer, Inc., Portland, Maine

Fig. 1

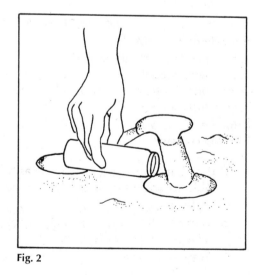

Fig. 2

pound of wax (unless it is already contained in the wax) and add the dye of your choice (see page 6 for instructions). If you want to refill the wells with a contrasting color wax, set some aside for this purpose at this time. At the last moment, add the scent (see page 7).

8. Pour the wax slowly into the sand mold.

9. After about 45 minutes, you will find that a well has formed in each of the rounded points of your triangle. Use a knitting needle or pencil to poke 2 holes in each well. Insert a wire-core wick in the center of each point and then refill the wells with hot wax, making sure that the wicks remain straight (see figure 4).

10. If you want a refillable candle, use short wicks. Then, after the inner holes have been burned, you can insert small votives.

11. When the candle has completely hardened, lift it out of the box and brush off the loose sand.

12. Dip the candle in and out of hot (240° F) clear wax to give the sand a glazed look (see page 10).

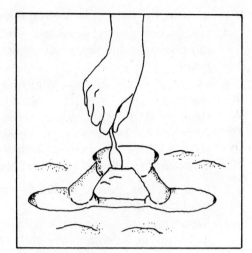

Fig. 3

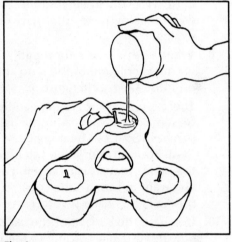

Fig. 4

FREE-FORM CANDLE*

Ingredients:
Wax: paraffin and stearic acid
Wick: wire-core
Dye: your choice and powdered
Scent: your choice
Sandbox
Coffee can or jar

1. Use whatever type of sand is easily available to you—sandblasting, construction, or beach.

2. Dampen the sand and pack it firmly into a large carton or dishpan.

3. Press the coffee can or jar into the sand

* Martin Products, Paterson, New Jersey

101

to make the basic hole. Lift the can out.

4. Using your fingers, poke and prod the sand to make the shape you desire (see figure 1).

5. Melt the wax, using the double-boiler method. When it is fully melted, add stearic acid (if it is not already in the wax) at the rate of 2 tablespoons per pound of wax. Add dye according to instructions on page 6. Finally add scent (see page 7).

6. Pour the wax, heated to 200°F, into the sand mold (see figure 2).

7. After about 45 minutes, the cooling wax will form an indentation or well on the surface. Use a knitting needle or pencil to poke 3 holes in the well. Insert a wire-core wick and refill the well with hot wax, making sure the wick remains straight.

8. When the wax has thoroughly cooled, lift the candle out of the sand and brush off loose sand, as in figure 3.

9. There are 2 versions to this candle: it can be semicoated with sand: that is, only in patches. Or it can be completely free of sand. You will find, when you lift it out of the sand, that it will be semicoated. If you want to remove the coating, dip the candle in hot water several times.

10. Decorate the surface of the candle with powdered dye according to the instructions on page 10.

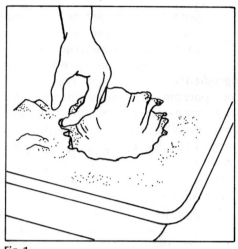

Fig. 1

Fig. 2

Fig. 3

BEACHCOMBER CANDLE*

Ingredients:
Wax: paraffin and stearic acid
Wick: wire-core
Dye: your choice and powdered
Scent: your choice
Sandbox
Bottle (3-inch diameter)
11 sticks of wood, 1 1/4-inch diameter by
  3 1/2 inches long

1. Use whatever sand is easily available to you—sandblasting, construction, or beach.

2. Dampen the sand and mound it up in a large carton or dishpan.

3. Take a rounded 3-inch-diameter bottle and press it firmly into the sand (see figure 1).

4. Cut sticks of dead wood to 1 1/4 inches in diameter by 3 1/2 inches long. Press them into the sand around the bottle (see figure 2).

5. Pack the sand firmly around the sticks.

6. Lift the bottle out of the center of the circle of sticks.

7. With a smaller-diameter bottle or a hammer, tap a firm base of 3 inches of sand in the center of the circle of sticks (see figure 3).

8. In order to make the candle as illustrated, you will need wax heated to a very hot 245°F. Since a double boiler limits you to a heat of 212°F, the wax for this candle must be melted in a pot directly over the heat. Be extremely careful when doing this to avoid burning or scorching the wax.

9. When the wax is fully melted, add stearic acid (if it is not already in the wax) at the rate of 2 tablespoons per pound of wax. It is not necessary to add dye to the wax, since the sticks will conceal most of the wax from view. If you do want to dye the wax, follow the instructions on page 6. At the last moment, add scent (see page 7).

10. Pour the wax into the center of the circle

* W. Spencer, Inc., Portland, Maine

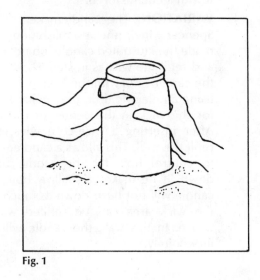

Fig. 1

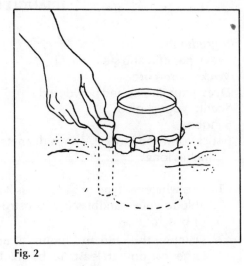

Fig. 2

103

of sticks. It must be poured at a bubbly and boiling 245°F, otherwise the wood may not stick to it.

11. About 45 minutes after pouring the wax, a well will form. Poke 3 holes in the well, using a pencil or knitting needle, and refill it with hot wax.

12. When the wax has completely hardened, lift the candle out of the box and brush off any loose sand.

13. Insert the wick with a heated skewer (see page 10). After the wick has dried firmly in place, dip the entire candle in a hot (240°F) clear wax bath (see page 10 and figure 4).

14. Sprinkle powdered dye from a shaker (see page 50) over the surface and glaze it with a butane torch.

15. **VARIATION:** The candlemakers of W. Spencer, Inc., the establishment that made the illustrated candle, do not poke and refill the well as in step 11. They let the candle cool with the well in it. Then, using an electric drill, they make a hole for the wick in the center of the well. After inserting a wire-core wick, they refill the well. This allows a candlemaker to control how far the candle burns down. If he makes a shallow hole, the candle will not burn down as much and the wick area can be refilled with a votive. In this way, the candle will last indefinitely.

Fig. 3

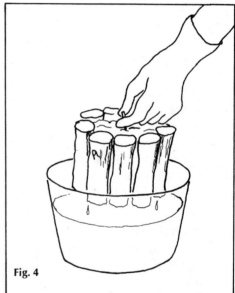

Fig. 4

TRIANGLE BEACHCOMBER CANDLE*

Ingredients:
Wax: paraffin and stearic acid
Wick: wire-core
Dye: your choice and powdered
Scent: your choice
Sandbox
6 sticks of wood, to 1 1/4-inch diameter by 7 inches long

1. Use whatever type of sand is easily available to you—sandblasting, construction, or beach.

2. Dampen the sand and mound it up in a large carton (at least 12 by 12 by 14

* W. Spencer, Inc., Portland, Maine

104

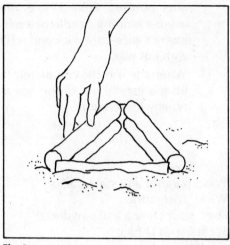

Fig. 1

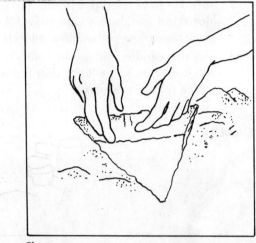

Fig. 2

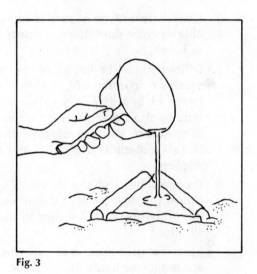

Fig. 3

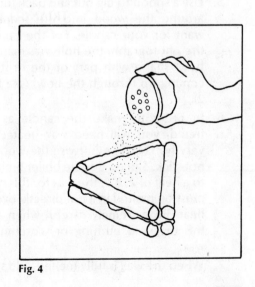

Fig. 4

inches) or dishpan.

3. Using your hands, dig out a roughly triangular hole (see figure 1).

4. You will need 6 pieces of dead wood for this candle, each piece 7 inches in length and 1 to 1 1/4 inches in diameter.

5. Press the wood, 2 pieces to each side, against the sand at the edges of the triangular hole (see figure 2).

6. Pack the sand firmly around the outside of the wood.

7. In order to make the candle as illustrated, you will need wax heated to a very hot 245° F, otherwise the wood will not stick. Since a double boiler limits you to a heat of 212° F, the wax for this candle must be melted in a pot directly over the heat. Be extremely careful when doing this to avoid burning or scorching the wax.

8. When the wax is fully melted, add stearic acid (if it is not already in the wax) at the rate of 2 tablespoons per pound of wax. It is not necessary to add dye to the wax, since the sticks will conceal most of the wax from view. If you do want to dye the wax, follow the instructions on page 6. Add scent at the last moment before pouring the wax (see page 7).

9. Pour the wax into the triangular hole. (see Figure 3).

10. As the wax cools, it contracts, forming a well or indentation in the surface. The well generally appears about 45 minutes

after pouring. Poke 3 holes in the well, using a knitting needle or a pencil. Then insert a wire-core wick and refill the well with hot wax.

11. When the wax has completely hardened, lift the candle out of the box and brush off any loose sand.

12. Sprinkle powdered dye on the surface as illustrated in figure 4 (see page 50) and glaze the colors with a butane torch.

13. Dip the candle into a hot (240°F) clear wax bath (see page 10) to coat the wood with a thin film of wax.

DRIFTWOOD CANDLE

Ingredients:
Wax: paraffin and stearic acid
Wick: wire-core
Dye: your choice and powdered
Scent: your choice
Sandbox
Driftwood

1. Use whatever type of sand is easily available to you—sandblasting, construction, or beach.

2. Driftwood can be found, of course, in a seashore community, either on the beach or in a shop. If you live in a city, inquire at a florist shop for information as to where you can obtain driftwood. Florists sometimes use it as a part of floral displays.

3. Dampen the sand and mound it up in a carton that will be large enough to hold the driftwood with 3 inches to spare on all sides.

4. Bury the driftwood and pack the sand around it (see figure 1).

5. Use a spoon to dig out and pack the sand around the wood into the shape you want for your candle. For the candle in the photograph, the hole was made in a bowl shape with part of the driftwood coming up through the bowl (see figure 2).

6. In order to make the candle as illustrated, you will need wax heated to a very hot 245°F, otherwise the wood will not stick. Since a double boiler limits you to a heat of 212°F, the wax for this candle must be melted in a pot directly over the heat. Be extremely careful when doing this to avoid burning or scorching the wax.

7. When the wax is fully melted, add stearic

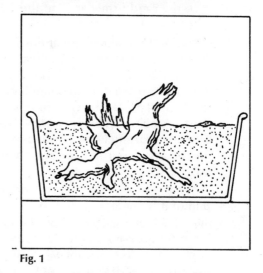

Fig. 1

acid (if it is not already in the wax) at the rate of 2 tablespoons per pound of wax. Add dye according to the instructions on page 6. At the last moment, add scent (see page 7).

8. Pour the wax (heated to 245°F) into the hole in the sand (see figure 3).

9. After about 45 minutes, you will find that

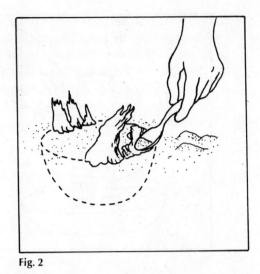

Fig. 2

Fig. 3

Fig. 4

the cooling wax has formed a well or indentation on the surface. Poke 3 holes in this well with a knitting needle or pencil and insert a wire-core wick. Then refill the well with hot wax. Continue poking and refilling as often as the well forms.

10. When the candle has completely hardened, lift it out of the box and brush off any loose sand.

11. Use shakers (as described on page 50) to sprinkle powdered dye over the surface of the candle. Carefully glaze the dye with a butane torch, taking care not to point the flame directly on the driftwood (see figure 4).

12. Do not dip this candle in hot wax, since the wood would lose its weathered appearance.

CLAY-CAST CANDLE

Ingredients:
Wax: paraffin and stearic acid
Wick: flat- or square-braided
Dye: your choice
Scent: your choice
Paper plate
Paper-towel tube
Water-base ceramic clay

1. Poke a small hole in the center of a paper plate. Center a paper towel tube over the hole.

2. Knead water-base ceramic clay until it is

107

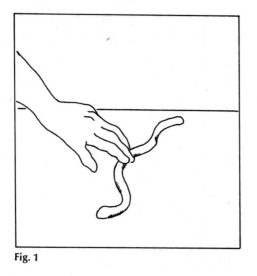

Fig. 1

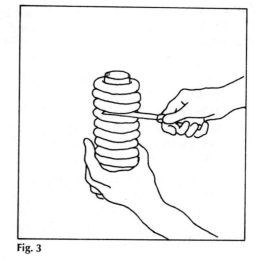

Fig. 2

Fig. 3

flexible. Roll it between your hands into 3/8-inch-thick ropes (see figure 1).

3. Coil the clay ropes around the tube, but not *too* tightly, since you will want to remove the tube later. Join the ends of the ropes by pressing them together (see figure 2).

4. Reinforce the base with extra clay.

5. Smooth the outside of the coils with a knife to seal the cracks (see figure 3).

6. Carefully lift the paper-towel tube out of the coiled clay.

7. Tie a knot in the end of the wick and thread the loose end through the hole in the bottom of the plate. Pull the wick up through the mold and center it by tying it to a pencil resting across the top of the mold.

8. Melt wax, using the double-boiler method. When it is fully melted, add stearic acid (if it is not already in the wax) at the rate of 2 tablespoons per pound of wax. Add dye according to the instructions on page 6, and at the last moment before pouring, add scent (see page 7).

9. Have some extra clay at hand to patch up any leaks that may develop when you pour the wax into the mold.

10. When the wax is 180°F, pour it slowly into the mold.

11. As the wax cools, it contracts and forms a well or indentation on the surface

Fig. 4

108

around the wick. When the well appears (about 45 minutes after pouring), poke 3 holes in it and refill it with hot wax. Do this as often as necessary.

12. When the wax has cooled completely, peel off the clay (see figure 4). If any clay remains clinging to the wax, scrub the candle gently with a brush and water. Since the clay is water-based, it will dissolve and wash away.

FREE-FORM CLAY-CAST CANDLE*

Ingredients:
Wax: paraffin and stearic acid
Wick: wire-core
Dye: your choice
Scent: your choice
Water-base ceramic clay
Bottle
Shallow box
Wax bath

* Corona International, Hackensack, New Jersey

1. Knead water-base ceramic clay until it is flexible.
2. Place the bottle in the center of a wad of clay and pack the clay thickly against its sides (see figure 1).
3. Remove the bottle. Use your hands to pull the clay into the freeform shape you desire (see figure 2).
4. Melt wax, using the double-boiler method. When it is fully melted, add stearic acid (if it is not already in the wax) at the rate of 2 tablespoons per pound of wax. Add dye according to the instructions on page 6. If you want to make a layered candle, as in the illustration, see page 88. Don't forget to add scent right before you pour wax (see page 7).
5. Place the clay mold in a shallow box and reinforce its base with extra clay. This is in case of leaks.
6. When the wax is 170°F, pour it slowly into the mold (see figure 3).
7. After about 45 minutes, you will notice that a well or indentation has formed on the surface of the cooling wax. Use a knitting needle or pencil to poke 3 holes in the well and insert a wire-core wick. Then refill the well with hot wax, making

Fig. 1

sure the wick remains straight. Continue poking and refilling as often as the well forms.

8. When the wax has completely cooled, pull the clay away from the candle. If any clay remains clinging to the wax, scrub the

109

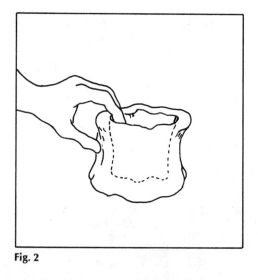

Fig. 2

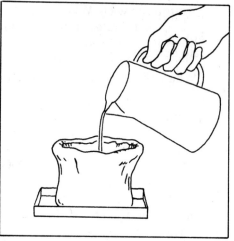

Fig. 3

Fig. 4

candle gently with a brush and water. Since the clay is water-based, it will dissolve and wash away.

9. To remove any imperfections and to add gloss to your candle, dip it in and out of hot (240°F) clear wax (see page 10—figure 4).

MULTICOLORED CARVED CANDLE

Ingredients:
Wax: low-melting-point (130°F) paraffin
Wick: square-braided
Dye: 3 colors (at least)
Scent: your choice
Plain dinner candle (optional)
Small sharp knife

1. There are 2 ways to make this candle: the first way is to start from scratch, that is, to begin with a length of wick and a pot of wax. The second way is to start with a plain white dinner candle as a core candle and dip it in the pot of wax.

2. Melt the wax, using the double-boiler

110

method. Do not add stearic acid.

3. Pour the liquid wax into at least 3 separate containers and add a different color dye to each (see page 6). Make sure the containers are large enough to permit you to dip in a core candle, if you decide on the second method of starting the candle (see step 1, above). At the last moment, add scent (see page 7).

4. Do not let the wax in the containers get hotter than 170°F. The cooler the wax, the more it will adhere to the candle.

5. When you use the first method, dip the length of wick quickly in and out of one of the containers of dyed wax. When you use the second method, do the same with the core candle (see figure 1).

6. Continue dipping until you have built up a noticeable layer of the dyed wax.

7. Let the candle cool until the wax on it is no longer tacky to the touch.

8. Then dip the candle into a different color (see figure 2) and continue with steps 5 and 6.

9. Continue this process with as many colors as you want until you have a rather fat concentric layered candle.

10. Let the candle cool. You can hasten this process by running cool water over the candle, then hanging it up by the wick.

11. When the candle has cooled, but is not yet hard, gouge out sections of the candle with a sharp knife so that you get a decorative effect, exposing the concentric colors (see figure 3).

12. **VARIATION:** Carve a scallop around the candle as an alternative to gouging it.

Fig. 1

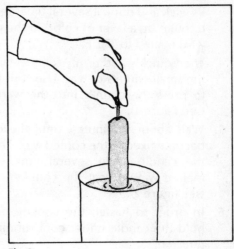
Fig. 2

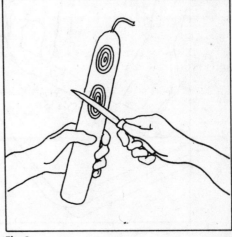
Fig. 3

CHUNK ROLLED CANDLE

Ingredients:
Wax: paraffin, and leftover bits of wax
Dye: your choice
Plain dinner candle
Cookie sheet

1. To make this candle, start a collection of leftover bits and chunks of wax—saved perhaps from previous candlemaking. Break the chunks into small pieces and spread them on a cookie sheet.

2. Melt wax, using the double-boiler method. Do not add stearic acid. When the wax is fully melted, add the dye of your choice (see page 6).

3. Hold a normal dinner candle or taper by its wick and dunk it several times (enough to build up a layer of color) in the melted wax, heated to 170° F.

4. Then quickly and firmly roll the candle in the small chunks of wax. Use your fingers to press the chunks into the warm wax (see figure 1).

5. Wait about 5 minutes, until the chunks become fixed in the cooled wax. Then dip the candle again several times in the melted wax to coat the chunks in place (see figure 2).

6. In order to hasten the cooling process, hold the candle under cool running water.

Fig. 2

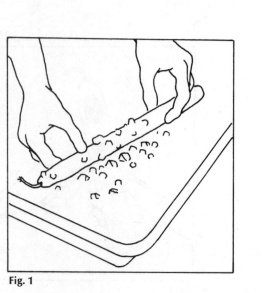

Fig. 1

CHANDELIER CANDLE*

Ingredients:
Wax: paraffin and stearic acid
Wick: wire-core
Dye: your choice and powdered
Scent: your choice
Gelatin mold
Electric drill
4   4 1/2-inch leather thongs

1. This candle was made in a tin gelatin mold from Mexico. It is an inexpensive mold and can be found, in large cities, in cookware supply or import shops. It isn't necessary, of course, for you to have the identical mold. Just pick a shape that will adapt itself to the chandelier idea.

2. Melt wax, using the double-boiler method. When it is fully melted, add stearic acid (if it is not already in the wax) at the rate of 2 tablespoons per pound of wax. Add the dye of your choice according to the instructions on page 6. (The candle in the illustration was made with undyed wax). At the last moment, add scent (see page 7).

3. Lightly grease the mold with cooking oil or silicone mold-release spray.

4. Slowly pour the wax, heated to 180°F, into the mold (see figure 1).

5. Let the mold stand for 1/2 minute to allow the air bubbles to rise, then carefully place it in a water bath of room-temperature water.

6. As the wax cools, it contracts, forming a well or indentation on the surface. About 45 minutes after pouring, the well will appear. Poke it 3 times with a knitting needle or pencil and refill with hot wax. Repeat this process as often as the well appears.

7. When the wax has cooled completely, remove it from the mold by gently pulling the edges of the mold away from the candle. Invert the mold over a padded surface, and the wax should fall out. If it stays stuck, drop the mold onto the padded surface from a height of a few

* W. Spencer, Inc., Portland, Maine

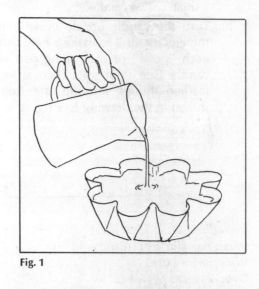

Fig. 1

inches. If still stuck, let it cool longer.

8. Follow the instructions for making dye shakers (on page 50) and sprinkle powdered dye on the top of the candle. Then use a butane torch to glaze the colors together. Turn the candle upside down and do the same thing for the bottom (see figure 2).

9. Since this will be a hanging candle, you

113

Fig. 2

Fig. 3

would not want a long wick that would burn all the way to the bottom of the candle. Use the electric drill or a heated skewer to make a short wick hole and insert a wire-core wick. Then, when the wick burns down, you can replace it with a small votive candle.

10. Turn the candle upside down and use the electric drill to make a hole through each "petal" or protruding part of the candle (see figure 3). Then string the leather thongs through the holes as shown in the drawing (see figure 4).

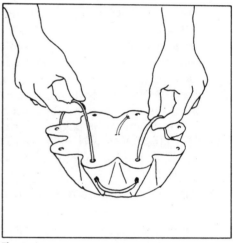

Fig. 4

MOOD CANDLE

Ingredients:
Wax: paraffin and stearic acid
Wick: wire-core
Dye: 2 colors
Scent: your choice
Medium-sized bowl
Small sharp knife

1. Melt wax, using the double-boiler method. When it has fully melted, add stearic acid (if it is not already in the wax) at the rate of 2 tablespoons per pound of wax.

2. Pour half of the wax into a separate container. Add a different color dye (see

114

page 6) to each half. Add scent to each container of wax only just before pouring (see page 7).

3. Pour one color of wax into the medium-sized bowl, filling it. The color used for this step in the candle illustrated was orange.

4. Wax cools from the outside to the inside; that is, the wax against the edge of the mold and along the top surface cools first, since it is closer to the cool air. The wax in the center takes the longest time to harden. For this candle, wait until 1/2-inch of wax has hardened against the side of the bowl before proceeding with the next step.

5. Use a small knife to cut a circle in the crust on the wax surface, leaving 1/2-inch border around the sides. Lift the wax circle away from the mold and pour out the liquid wax that is inside. You now have a 1/2-inch shell of wax (see figure 1).

6. Let the shell of wax stand in the bowl for 5 minutes, or until it is no longer runny. Then use the small knife to cut any pattern you want into the wax shell: scallops, curlicues, stripes, and so on. Lift out portions of the shell in making your pattern (see figure 2).

7. Now let the design in the wax cool until it is no longer soft.

8. Reheat the second color of wax to 160°F and slowly pour it into the bowl. The color used for this step in the illustration was blue. This wax will fill in the spaces in your pattern, making a two-colored candle. Fill the bowl to the top (see figure 3).

9. After about 45 minutes, a well will form in the surface of the wax. Use a knitting needle or a pencil to poke 3 holes in the well and refill it with hot wax. Do this as often as the well appears.

10. When the wax has cooled completely, invert the bowl over a padded surface and the candle should release. If it doesn't, let it cool some more.

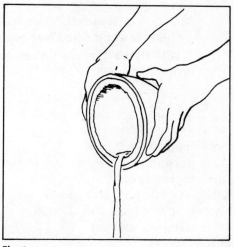

Fig. 1

Fig. 2

Fig. 3

11. Insert the wick (the top of the candle being the rounded side), using the heated skewer method (see page 10).
12. **VARIATION:** This candle can look very attractive as a chandelier, surrounded by leather thongs or a macramé sling. In this case, insert the wick into the flat side of the candle.

WATER CANDLE

Ingredients:
Wax: paraffin
Dye: your choice
Tubular candle for a core candle
Kitchen bowl (5- to 6-inch diameter)
Wide, deep wastebasket
Rubber gloves

1. Purchase a tall (12-inch) tubular candle to use as a core or base. The best results in a water candle occur if the core candle is 1 1/2 to 2 inches in diameter.
2. Melt wax, using the double-boiler method, to 180°F. Do not add stearic acid. Add the dye of your choice (see page 6). For the candle in the photograph, we dyed the wax to match the core candle, but a contrasting color can look very attractive.
3. Fill a deep, wide-mouthed container, such as a metal or plastic wastebasket, with lukewarm water. The container should be deeper than the height of the core candle.
4. Place the core candle upright in a small kitchen bowl (5 to 6 inches in diameter). Pour approximately 1/2 inch of wax into the bottom of the bowl.
5. Let this wax harden, forming a base to hold the core candle in place (see illustration).
6. This candle can be rather messy in the making, so place the container of water in an area that won't be damaged by puddles of water. Or surround the container with towels. Put on rubber gloves.
7. Pour 2 more inches of the colored wax (at 180°F) into the bowl.
8. Then, grasping the bowl with both hands, submerge the bowl and core candle into the water container. Turn the bowl as you lower it to gain a spiral

effect. The liquid wax will rise in the water and swirl around the core candle.
9. If you don't get an effective-looking creation the first time, add more liquid wax to the bowl and repeat step 8.
10. When the wax has fully colored, remove the candle from the bowl. You will find it has a built-in base.

116

SHELL CANDLE

Ingredients:
Wax: paraffin and stearic acid
Wick: wire-core plus wick tab
Dye: 2 colors
Scent: your choice
Circular mold
Eggbeater or fork

1. Use a circular paper or cardboard mold, such as an oatmeal or ice-cream container, for this candle. The candle in the photograph was made in a round salt box. Lightly grease the mold with cooking oil or silicone mold-release spray.

2. Melt wax, using the double-boiler method. When it is fully melted, add stearic acid (if it is not already in the wax) at the rate of 2 tablespoons per pound of wax. If you decide not to use 2 types of wax with differing melting points for this candle, set 1/2 of the wax aside in a separate container at this point.

3. Add dye, according to the instructions on page 6), to the wax. If you have poured 1/2 of the wax into a separate container (see step 2), add a different color dye to each half. Add scent just before pouring (see page 7).

4. Slowly pour the wax (at 160°F) into the mold, which is held at a tilt while pouring.

5. Allow the wax to cool just enough so that a shell of hardened wax forms around the sides and the bottom of the mold. A crust should appear on the surface.

6. Use a small knife to cut a circle in the crust, leaving about 1/8 inch of hardened wax around the edge (see figure 1).

7. Lift the circle away and pour out the liquid wax. You will be left with a colored wax shell.

8. At this point, either you will use the wax you have poured into a separate container (see steps 2 and 3) or you will melt low-melting-point wax (130°F melting point) and add a second color of dye. Pour this wax into a deep, wide-mouthed bowl.

Fig. 1

Fig. 2

9. Let the wax in the bowl cool until a skin (not a thick crust) appears on the surface.

10. Using an eggbeater (or, if you don't have one, a fork), whip the wax until it becomes fluffy and foamy.

11. Place a wire-core wick with a weight at the bottom (wick tab) into the shell of wax, making sure you have centered it. Fasten the top of the wick to a pencil and center the pencil across the top of the mold.

12. Scoop 1/2 inch of the whipped wax into the shell. Let it harden, forming a support for the wick.

13. Fill the shell with the whipped wax (see figure 2). When the wax has hardened, tear off the paper mold.

14. When the candle is lit, the whipped wax in the center will burn, leaving the shell empty and ready to be refilled with more wax (with another wick), if you desire.

INDEX

INDEX

Acrylic-painted candle, 82
Aluminum-foil candles, 22 - 25. *See also* under specific names.
Aluminum-foil cube candle, 23 - 24
Aluminum-foil free-form candle, 22 - 23
Aluminum-foil sand candle, 24 - 25
Appliqué candle, 84
Ashtray molded candle, 30 - 31
Autumn leaves candle, 72
Autumn tomato candle, 70 - 71

Bayberry wax, 3
Beachcomber candle, 103 - 4
Beeswax, 3
    as additive for hardening wax, 4
Birthday cake candle, 61 - 62
Birthday clown candle, 60 - 61

Candelilla wax, 3
    as additive for hardening wax, 3
Candlemaking
    achieving opacity in, 4, 5
    hot wax bath in, 10 - 11
    materials for, 3, 4, 7
    methods of inserting wick, 10
    polishing in, 11, 13
    precautions in, 13 - 14

problems in, 9, 12 - 13
steps in, 7 - 11
unmolding, 10, 12
water bath in, 9 - 10, 12
wax pouring in, 7, 9, 12, 13, 14
Candles
additives to improve appearance and quality in, 5
container. *See* Container candles.
definition of, 3
kinds of, 4, 6. *See also* under specific names.
methods of scenting, 7
molded. *See* Molded candles.
well in. *See* Well.
Carnauba wax, 3
as additive for hardening wax, 3
Carved clay candle, 37 - 40
Chandelier candle, 113 - 14
Chip-carved candle, 41 - 42
Christmas tree candles, 62 - 64
Chunk candle, 92 - 93
Chunk candles, 92 - 93, 112. *See also* under specific names.
Chunk rolled candle, 112
Clay-cast candle, 107 - 9
Clay-cast candles, 37 - 40, 93 - 95, 107 - 10. *See also* under specific names.
Cloves, oil of, 7
Coaster candle, 36 - 37
Coffee can sand candle, 98 - 99
Coiled cube candle, 47 - 48
Coloring. *See* Dyeing.
Concentric-colors candle, 90 - 91
Container candles, 4, 6
Cookie-cutter layered candle, 48 - 49
Corrugated candle, 18 - 19
Crystals, 13
as additives to improve appearance and quality, 5, 9
Cut-glass candle, 42 - 43

Decoupage candle, 85
Decoupage candles, 83 - 87. *See also* under specific names.
Doily candle, 83
Double-wick milk-carton candle, 17 - 18
Driftwood candle, 106 - 7
Dripless candles, 6
Dripping, 6
Dyeing, 6 - 7

methods of, 6. *See also* under specific methods.
Dyes, 4, 5, 6, 7, 9
kinds of, 6. *See also* under specific kind.

Easter egg candle, 69 - 70
Edged candle, 45
Etched candle, 40 - 41

Flat-braided wick, 6
Flower candles, 57 - 59

Garden flare, 75
Gelatin-mold mushroom, 28 - 30
Glass-bottle candle, 10, 12, 21 - 22

Hand-dipped tapers, 34 - 35
Hand-rolled candle, 51 - 52
Hardening wax. *See* Wax, methods of hardening.
Homemade coloring agents, 6
Hot wax bath, 10 - 11
Household-item candles, 15 - 33. *See also* under specific names.

Ice-cream-soda candle, 76
Ice-cube candle, 95 - 96

Jack-o'-lantern candle, 72 - 73

Kitchen-mold floating candle, 27 - 28

Lavender, oil of, 7
Layered candle, 88 - 90
Layered chunk candle, 93 - 95

Marbleized candle, 52 - 53
Melting point. *See* Wax, melting point of.
Metal-core wick, 6, 13
Metal molds, 10, 12
Milk-carton candle, 8, 15 - 17
Modern candles, 88 - 118. *See also* under specific names.
Molded candles, 3 - 4, 7, 8, 27 - 31
improving gloss in, 5
Molds, 10
kinds of, 8, 10, 12, 27 - 31. *See also* under specific molds.
preparation of, 8
problems with, 9, 11, 13
Mood candle, 114 - 16

Multicolored carved candle, 110 - 11
Mushroom candle, 49 - 51

Octopus candle, 99
Oils, 6
    essential; kinds of, 7. *See also* under specific kinds.
    petroleum, 4
    scented. *See* Oils, essential.
    use in candlemaking, 3, 13
Oil-soluble dyes
    color buds, 6
    liquid, 6
    powdered, 6
Ornate candles, 34 - 43. *See also* under specific names.

Painted candles, 78 - 82. *See also* under specific names.
Paper-tube mold, 10
Paraffin
    commercial, 4
    household, 4
    nature of, 4
Patchouli, oil of, 7
Plastic-bag candle, 25 - 26
Plastic-flower candle, 86 - 87
Polishing, in candlemaking, 11
Polyethylene, 5

Rolled candles, 46 - 47, 51 - 55. *See also* under specific names.
Rolled strobe candle, 53 - 54
Rolled strobe candle with petals, 54 - 55
Rolled tube candle, 46 - 47

Sand candles, 8, 24 - 25, 96 - 101. *See also* under specific names.
Scent, 7, 9, 13
    kinds of, 7
Shell candle, 117 - 18
Snowman candle, 64 - 66
Special-occasion candles, 60 - 77. *See also* under specific names.
Spermaceti, 3
Sponge-painted candle, 80 - 81
Square-braided wick, 6
Stearic acid, 11, 12, 13
    as additive for achieving opacity in wax, 4, 5
    as additive for hardening wax, 4, 9

Stearine. *See* Stearic acid.
Strobe candles, 53 - 55, 77. *See also* under specific names.
Swirl-painted candle, 81

Tapers, 6, 34 - 35
Through-and-through coloring, 6
Triangle beachcomber candle, 104 - 6
Triangle sand candle, 100 - 1
Two-wick cardboard-box candle, 20 - 21

Unmolding in candlemaking, 10, 11

Valentine candle, 66 - 67
Valentine heart candle, 68

Waffle-iron candle, 32 - 33
Water bath, use in candlemaking, 9 - 10, 12, 13
Water candle, 116
Water-soluble dyes, 6
Wax, 3, 4, 6, 14
    additives used to harden, 3, 4
    kinds of, 3, 4. *See also* under specific names.
    melting point of, 3, 4, 7, 11
    methods of hardening, 4, 10
    methods of making, 3
    methods of melting, 8, 13
    pouring in candlemaking, 9
    problems with, 12, 13
    use in candlemaking, 7, 9
Wax-dripped candle, 79 - 80
Wax-painted candles, 78 - 79
Wax-sheet candles, 44 - 59. *See also* under specific names.
Well, 7, 10, 12, 13
Wick, 3, 4, 5, 6, 11
    as aid to proper burning, 5
    choosing correct size, 5 - 6
    kinds of, 6, 13. *See also* under specific names.
    methods of inserting, 8 - 9, 10
    problems with, 13
    use in scenting, 7
Wicking, definition of, 6
    methods of making, 6
Wintergreen, oil of, 7
Wire-core wick. *See* Metal-core wick.
Witch hat, 74
Wrapped candle, 56